THE UNIV!
WIN~

# Spor~ ~y ~sure

London: H M S O

Researched and written by Reference Services, Central Office of Information.

© Crown copyright 1994
Applications for reproduction should be made to HMSO.
First published 1994

ISBN 0 11 701740 X

HMSO publications are available from:

**HMSO Publications Centre**
(Mail, fax and telephone orders only)
PO Box 276, London SW8 5DT
Telephone orders 071-873 9090
General enquiries 071-873 0011
(queuing system in operation for both numbers)
Fax orders 071-873 8200

**HMSO Bookshops**
49 High Holborn, London WC1V 6HB    071-873 0011
Fax 071-873 8200 (counter service only)
258 Broad Street, Birmingham B1 2HE    021-643 3740    Fax 021-643 6510
33 Wine Street, Bristol BS1 2BQ
0272 264306    Fax 0272 294515
9-21 Princess Street, Manchester M60 8AS    061-834 7201    Fax 061-833 0634
16 Arthur Street, Belfast BT1 4GD    0232 238451    Fax 0232 235401
71 Lothian Road, Edinburgh EH3 9AZ    031-228 4181    Fax 031-229 2734

**HMSO's Accredited Agents**
(see Yellow Pages)
and through good booksellers

# Contents

# Acknowledgments

This book has been compiled with the co-operation of a number of organisations, including other government departments and sports governing bodies. The Central Office of Information would like to thank in particular the Department of National Heritage, the Sports Council, The Scottish Office, the Welsh Office, the Northern Ireland Office and the Department for Education.

## Cover Photograph Credit

Associated Press

# Introduction

More than half the population of Britain[1] regularly takes part in some form of sporting activity. Swimming, snooker and keep fit/aerobics are some of the most popular participation sports, and many others are played by a growing number of participants. The most popular leisure activities, however, are those based in the home and range from DIY to watching television.

Government funding for sport is mostly channelled through the Sports Councils, which make grants to the governing bodies of sport and other national and local organisations. The Councils work closely with the Government in implementing sports policies and have the general aim of increasing the opportunities for sport within Britain. Local authorities are the main providers of sports facilities.

Individual sports are organised by independent governing bodies, which are responsible for a wide range of matters, including drawing up rules and holding events. The needs of Britain's top performers are catered for at the Sports Councils' National Sports Centres, which also run courses for the local community.

Sport benefits considerably from the various forms of sponsorship and funding which are available. These include widespread commercial sponsoring and the Government's new Business Sponsorship Scheme for the development of sports at a local level.

The Government's policy statement *Sport and Active Recreation*, published in 1991 (see Further Reading), emphasises

[1] The term 'Britain' is used informally in this book to mean the United Kingdom of Great Britain and Northern Ireland; 'Great Britain' comprises England, Wales and Scotland.

the Government's aim to encourage greater participation in sport from an early age. Physical education has now been incorporated into the National Curriculum for England and Wales and the Government is encouraging partnerships between schools and the local community.

Areas of concern for sport in recent years include spectator safety at sports grounds and drug abuse in sport. Following publication of the Taylor Report in 1990, the Government introduced a number of measures to improve crowd safety and these have also been successful in reducing crowd violence. Drug abuse in sport is monitored by stringent testing of competitors both in and out of competition.

At international level Britain can boast more than 80 world champions in over 30 sports. Recent success at major international championships includes five gold medals at the 1992 Barcelona Olympics and three gold medals at the 1993 World Athletics Championships.

The major sporting events of the year include the FA (Football Association) Challenge Cup Final, the Wimbledon lawn tennis championships and the Open Golf Championship, all of which are watched by large crowds and even larger television audiences. The biggest television audience for a single event in 1992 was achieved by the Grand National steeplechase, which attracted over 16 million viewers. Other sports which draw large TV viewing figures are football, athletics, snooker and boxing.

Following the introduction of direct broadcasting by satellite (DBS) and the greater availability of cable, the amount of televised coverage has increased substantially. Important sporting occasions ('listed events'), such as the Olympic Games, may not be shown exclusively by DBS or cable and must be made generally available to television viewers.

As well as being a popular pastime, sport is a major industry in Britain. In addition to the professional sportsmen and women, over 450,000 are employed in the provision of sports clothing, publicity, ground and club maintenance and other activities connected with sport. In total an estimated £9,750 million is spent on sport annually in Britain.

# Participation

An improvement in facilities and an increase in leisure time have helped to encourage more and more people to take part in sport. Levels of participation have also been boosted by a growing awareness of the importance of regular exercise for good health, which has resulted in an upsurge of interest in keep fit and other forms of aerobic exercise.

It is estimated that 29 million people over the age of 16 regularly take part in sport or other forms of exercise. The *General Household Survey 1990* [2] reveals that:

—65 per cent of those interviewed had taken part in at least one sporting activity during the four weeks before interview, compared with 61 per cent in 1987;

—men were more likely than women to have participated in sport (73 per cent of men as against 57 per cent of women);

—keep fit/yoga was the only sporting activity with a significantly higher participation rate among women than among men;

—eight out of the top ten activities were common to both sexes, with football and golf appearing only on the men's list, and ten-pin bowls and badminton featuring only in the women's top ten; and

—for most sports, participation declined with age (the participation rate was highest, at 87 per cent, among those aged 16 to 19 and lowest, at 31 per cent, among those aged 70 or over).

[2] Office of Population Censuses and Surveys. HMSO, £18.50.
ISBN 0 11 691385 1.

# Most Popular Participation Sports for Men and Women*

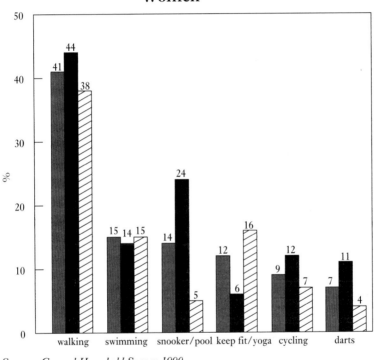

Source: *General Household Survey 1990.*
* Percentage participating in the four weeks before interview.

▓ Total ■ Men ▨ Women

Sport is becoming increasingly popular, but the most popular leisure activities of all are those based in the home. These range from physical activities, such as gardening and DIY, to less active pastimes, such as watching television and listening to the radio (see Table 1).

## Table 1: Participation in Home-based Leisure Activities

%*

|  | 1977 | 1980 | 1983 | 1986 | 1987 | 1990 |
|---|---|---|---|---|---|---|
| Watching television | 97 | 98 | 98 | 98 | 99 | 99 |
| Visiting or entertaining friends and relatives | 91 | 91 | 91 | 94 | 95 | 96 |
| Listening to the radio | 87 | 88 | 87 | 86 | 88 | 89 |
| Listening to records or tapes | 62 | 64 | 63 | 67 | 73 | 76 |
| Reading books | 54 | 57 | 56 | 59 | 60 | 62 |
| Gardening | 42 | 43 | 44 | 43 | 46 | 48 |
| DIY | 35 | 37 | 36 | 39 | 43 | 43 |
| Dressmaking, needlework or knitting | 29 | 28 | 27 | 27 | 27 | 23 |

Source: *General Household Survey 1990.*
* Percentage participating in the four weeks before interview.

## Women and Sport

A major effort was made in the 1980s to narrow the gap between men's and women's participation in sport. This resulted in an increase of 1 million in the number of women taking part in sport between 1987 and 1990, according to the *General Household Survey.* The numbers participating in 'physical contact' sports, such as football and rugby, are also increasing, and more women now play traditionally male-dominated sports, such as snooker and billiards. Sports and physical activities associated with fitness and healthy lifestyles are particularly favoured by women, with high rates of participation in swimming, keep fit and aerobics.

During the 1990s emphasis has switched to encouraging women to adopt leadership roles, such as coaches, officials and administrators. Efforts to promote coaching opportunities have been made by the Sports Councils, the National Coaching Foundation (see p. 20) and the Women's Sports Foundation (WSF—see below). In 1993 the Sports Council brought together 65 representatives from all areas of sport in England to discuss its consultation document on women and sport, published in 1992 (see Further Reading). Action agreed at the meeting will be published in the Sports Council's National Framework for Action on Women and Sport.

Many sports have separate governing bodies for women, and competitive events are normally organised in divisions for men and women. One notable exception is equestrianism, where women riders compete on equal terms with men. Mixed events in which men and women take part together are traditional in sports such as tennis, badminton and ice skating.

Netball is the main sport played predominantly by women. Other sports often played by girls at school include tennis, badminton, athletics, hockey, lacrosse, swimming and gymnastics.

**Women's Sports Foundation**

The WSF was founded in 1984 by a group of women working in sport who were concerned about the lack of opportunities for women in sport and recreation. Its main aims are to represent the views of the many women involved in sport and to seek ways of improving their status. With Sports Council funding, the WSF promotes the establishment of women in sports groups throughout Britain and seeks to co-operate with sports and education organisations. In 1986 it initiated the Sportswomen of the Year Awards and in 1992 it launched a nationwide awards scheme for girls and young women between the ages of 11 and 19. The scheme aims to encourage more young women to participate in sport and to pursue sporting careers.

The 1993 Awards Scheme offered a total of £50,000 in awards and was launched through schools, youth clubs, leisure centres, and sporting clubs and associations, with the backing of the Sports Council. Awards of between £500 and £1,000 were made under three categories: individual; team/club/community programme; and coach. The three overall category winners received an additional £1,000, and there were also two £5,000 awards for the Young Disabled Sportswoman of the Year and the Young Sportswoman of the Year.

## Ethnic Minorities

The Sports Council is actively encouraging local authorities to become more sensitive to the needs of minority groups in their communities. For example, in Yorkshire a network of contacts has been created within the black communities to involve ethnic minorities in cricket. This has increased the number of black cricket coaches and the numbers of young black people taking part in the game. The project is now being extended to other sports.

Many sports have already been successful in attracting large numbers of participants from the ethnic minorities. Athletics, for example, has a strong black representation, and at international level black athletes account for more than 30 per cent of the national squad. In boxing the participation rate is even higher. About half of all professional boxers licensed in Great Britain are black, and at July 1993 there were six black British champions. Other sports with a strong representation of ethnic minorities at all levels of competition include football, rugby union and rugby league.

## Young People

Physical education, including organised games, is part of the curriculum of all state-maintained schools. Playing fields must be available for pupils over the age of eight, and most secondary schools have a gymnasium. Opportunities out of school are organised by a wide range of organisations, such as local authorities and local sports clubs.

Special programmes of activity for young people are run by the governing bodies of individual sports, while the four Sports Councils organise local and national initiatives to encourage more young people to take part in sport out of school. In March 1993 the Sports Council launched a new policy document—*Young People and Sport*—which sets out a number of objectives to ensure a co-ordinated development of sport for young people. The document recommends better training of those working with young people, and provides action guidelines for governing bodies, sports clubs, local authorities, schools and the youth service to implement programmes to benefit young people's sport.

## Government's Objectives

The Government's policies and priorities were outlined in December 1991 in a sports policy statement—*Sport and Active Recreation* (see Further Reading). The Government's primary objectives are to:

—ensure that physical education takes its proper place in the school curriculum and that pupils participate regularly in sport and physical exercise (see p. 48);

—promote physical exercise and participation in sport and active recreation by adults, giving support where appropriate to the provision of facilities and of opportunities for participation;

—help participants in sport to achieve higher standards of performance and to enable those with the potential to excel to do so;

—encourage better use of local authority and school sports facilities, and partnership with the private sector in the provision and management of sports facilities (see p. 50);

—promote sport for people with disabilities and to encourage the greater integration of able-bodied and disabled people in sporting activities (see p. 39);

—promote fair play, supported by an effective, independent drug-testing regime (see p. 59);

—promote safety at sports grounds (see p. 54); and

—further the interests of British sport internationally.

The Government also intends to develop sport at the 'grass roots' level by encouraging business sponsorship (see p. 42).

# Organisation and Administration

Responsibility for government policy on sport and active recreation in England has rested with the Secretary of State for National Heritage since the creation of the Department of National Heritage in April 1992.[3] The Secretaries of State for Wales, Scotland and Northern Ireland are responsible for sport in their countries. In Northern Ireland the Department of Education makes direct grants towards the capital cost of facilities to local authorities and voluntary sports bodies.

Responsibility for the organisation and promotion of sport is largely decentralised, and many sport and recreation facilities are provided by local authorities. The Countryside Commission has specific recreation responsibilities, and other bodies, such as the Forestry Commission, provide recreational amenities in addition to their main functions. The main mechanism by which the Government directly channels financial assistance to sport, however, is through the Sports Councils. This 'arm's length' principle of funding safeguards the long-established independence of sports organisations in Britain.

## Sports Councils

The Sports Councils, appointed and directly funded by the Government, are the Government's principal advisers on sporting

[3] Other responsibilities of the Department of National Heritage include the arts, public libraries, local museums and galleries, tourism, heritage, broadcasting and the National Lottery.

matters. The Government works closely with them in implementing its sports policies.

## Structure

There are four Sports Councils:

—the Sports Council (for general matters affecting Great Britain and specifically English matters);

—the Sports Council for Wales;

—the Scottish Sports Council; and

—the Sports Council for Northern Ireland.

The Councils make grants for sports development, coaching and administration to the governing bodies of sports and other national organisations, and administer the National Sports Centres (see p. 27). Grants and loans are also made to voluntary organisations, local authorities and commercial organisations to help them provide sports facilities. In 1993-94 the Councils are allocating government funds amounting to approximately £67 million.

## Support for Facilities

Facilities receiving support from the Sports Councils include sports halls, indoor swimming pools, intensive-use pitches, indoor tennis halls and school facilities.

One of the Sports Council's most significant schemes—the Indoor Tennis Initiative (ITI)—is a major building programme to increase the availability of indoor tennis courts. Launched in 1986, the ITI was initially intended as a five-year programme to develop British tennis from the grass roots and to make tennis more accessible to the general public. The objectives are to establish a network of 50 local indoor tennis centres, through grant-aid of up to one-third of capital costs, and to maximise the use of outdoor courts through coaching and development programmes.

Twenty-one centres have been developed in England during Phase I of the programme, providing 87 indoor courts and 90 accompanying outdoor courts. Sports Council investment of £1.6 million was augmented by £3.8 million from the Lawn Tennis Association/All England Club and £9.6 million from other partners. Phase II, which is targeted at inner city areas and with higher levels of Council grant, has now started, with 12 of the 29 targeted projects at planning or design stages.

A Sports Council grant of £3 million contributed towards the costs of building the National Indoor Arena in Birmingham, which was formally opened in 1991. The arena has a seating capacity of 10,000 and has been designed and built at a cost of £50.6 million. It is run by the local authority and is designed to provide a world-class facility for the staging of international events as well as first-class facilities for the local community. In 1993 it staged the World Badminton Championships and in 1995 the World Netball Championships will be held there.

The Council has agreed to provide £1.5 million towards the development of a National Hockey Stadium at Milton Keynes. It has also identified requirements for national bowls facilities and has drawn up plans for a National Ice Training Centre. There are also plans to establish a National Movement and Dance Centre.

A total of 551 capital grants were awarded in 1991–92 by the regional offices of the Sports Council to a value of £11.5 million. This was boosted by a contribution of £1.5 million from commercial sponsors. The grants were distributed as follows: 393 to voluntary clubs, 113 to local authorities, and 45 to commercial undertakings. The projects included:

—8 swimming pools;

—25 sports halls;

—52 intensive-use pitches;

—26 multi-purpose games areas; and

—111 specialist facilities.

The Sports Council for Wales contributed over £175,000 in capital grants to local sports organisations in 1991–92.

In Scotland some £300,000 was contributed by the Scottish Sports Council towards the construction of the National Water-Ski Centre at Town Loch, Dunfermline, which opened in 1991. The Centre is expected to improve competition standards and to generate increased participation in water-skiing at all levels. The Scottish Sports Council also contributed £150,000 towards Scotland's first specialist equestrian centre, which was established in 1992 at Devon Park, Central Region.

The four Sports Councils are also concerned with preserving and extending recreational and sporting access to the countryside.

**Development of Sport**

Strategies for the development of sport have been drawn up by the four Sports Councils. The aims of these strategies are broadly to ensure that:

—all young people have the opportunity to acquire basic sports skills;

—everyone has the opportunity to take part in sport and active recreation of their choice;

—everyone with the interest and ability has the opportunity to improve their standard of performance in sport and fulfil their potential; and

—everyone with the interest and ability has the opportunity to reach the highest standards of sporting excellence.

A large proportion of the Sports Councils' budgets is directed at increasing participation by the general public. The Councils are concentrating in particular on raising participation rates among the young, inner city dwellers, people with disabilities (see p. 36) and other groups experiencing difficulties in gaining access to sporting opportunities.

A national strategic approach for Scottish sport was recently set out by the Scottish Sports Council. Sport 2000 aims to introduce 250,000 people to sport by the end of the decade and to target specific areas for development. It also intends to make sports more accessible to those groups which in the past have found it difficult to participate.

In May 1993 the Sports Council launched a new document—*Sport in the Nineties: New Horizons* (see Further Reading)—which sets out its vision for sport for the next five years. The document highlights the needs of Britain's top sportsmen and women and recommends:

—the provision of additional training camps, an overseas warm-weather training centre and enhanced support services in coaching, sports medicine and sports science (see p. 23);

—additional grants, ideally disbursed through the Sports Aid Foundation (see p. 43), to compensate athletes for expenses incurred while engaged in intensive training; and

—the phased building of key national sports facilities and a network of regional centres of excellence.

## Local Authorities

Local authorities are the main providers of basic sport and recreation facilities for the local community. In England local authorities manage over 1,500 indoor centres, largely built in the last 20 years, as well as numerous outdoor amenities. The facilities provided include parks, lakes, playing fields, sports halls, tennis courts, golf courses, swimming pools, gymnasiums and sports centres catering for a wide range of activities.

There has been a rapid growth in the provision of artificial pitches—largely for hockey—and a similar increase in the number of leisure pools, which offer wave machines, waterfalls, jacuzzis and other leisure equipment. Gross annual expenditure by local authorities on sport and recreation amounts to over £1,000 million in England alone.

In its 1991 policy statement the Government says that local authorities should:

—encourage greater use of their assets;

—work in partnership with the private sector and the local community for the improvement of existing facilities and the provision of new ones;

—work with voluntary organisations, sports clubs and the education service to harness available local skills and to increase participation and improve performance; and

—ensure in most rural areas, in their role as planning authorities, that a proper balance is achieved between the interests of sport and outdoor recreation, and those of conservation.

The Government has recommended that in the inner cities resources should be directed towards the funding of sports development officers, who would be responsible for ensuring the better use of recreational facilities by the local community.

## Competitive Tendering

The Government has instituted competitive tendering for the management of local authority sports and leisure facilities to make them more cost-effective and responsive to consumer demand. School and college facilities are exempted from competition, and councils retain controls over pricing, admission and opening hours. The Government believes that compulsory competitive tendering helps to stimulate a positive review of local authority practices and improved efficiency in leisure management.

## National Sports Associations

The Central Council of Physical Recreation (CCPR) is a non-governmental voluntary association in England whose membership consists of governing bodies of sport and other organisations with an interest in sport and physical recreation. Similar bodies in Scotland, Wales and Northern Ireland are the Scottish Sports Association, the Welsh Sports Association and the Northern Ireland Council of Physical Recreation (NICPR). The primary aim of these bodies is to represent the interests of their members to the appropriate national and local authorities, including the Sports Councils, from which they receive funding. Award schemes run by the associations include the CCPR's Community Sports Leaders Award Scheme and the NICPR's Service to Sport Awards.

The largest of the four associations is the CCPR, which comprises 200 British bodies and over 60 English associations. In recent years the CCPR has set up a number of sports bodies, including the Institute of Sports Sponsorship (ISS—see p. 42) and the Institute of Professional Sport (IPS). The ISS comprises some 80 major British companies that sponsor sport and aims to develop sponsorship at local, national and international level. The IPS comprises representatives from 11 sports associations and seeks to protect the welfare of professional sportsmen and women.

The CCPR has published a code of conduct for sport, *Fair Play in Sport—A Charter* (see Further Reading), which has achieved widespread support. Over 75 governing bodies of sport and recreation in Britain and more than 20 international sports bodies have pledged a commitment to its terms.

## British Sports Forum

The sports associations of Wales, Scotland and Northern Ireland, the CCPR and the British Olympic Association (see p. 22) have recently come together in the British Sports Forum. The purpose of this body is to present the united voice of the non-governmental sports sector, both domestically and internationally. The Sports Council has pledged its full support to this development, which is also welcomed by the Government.

## Sports Governing Bodies

Individual sports are run by over 400 independent governing bodies, whose functions usually include drawing up rules, holding events, regulating membership, selecting and training national teams and promoting international links. There are also organisations representing people who take part in more informal physical recreation, such as walking and cycling. The majority of the sports clubs in Britain belong to the appropriate governing body. The clubs are eligible for Sports Council grant aid towards the provision of facilities.

## Sports Clubs

A wide variety of recreational facilities are provided by local sports clubs. Some cater for indoor recreation, but more common are those providing sports grounds, particularly for cricket, football, rugby, hockey, tennis and golf. Estimates suggest that there are some 150,000 sports clubs in Britain, with about 6.5 million members. Many clubs linked to business firms cater for sporting activities. Commercial facilities include tenpin bowling centres, ice and roller-skating rinks, squash courts, golf courses and driving ranges, riding stables, marinas and, increasingly, fitness centres. In all, the private sector owns and runs some 500 major sports facilities.

## Countryside Bodies

The Countryside Commission (for England), the Countryside Council for Wales (CCW) and Scottish Natural Heritage (SNH) are responsible for conserving and improving the natural beauty and amenity of the countryside, and for encouraging the provision and improvement of facilities for open-air recreation.[4]

The countryside agencies give financial assistance to public, private and voluntary organisations carrying out countryside conservation, recreation and amenity projects. Activities aided by these agencies include the provision by local authorities and private bodies of country parks and picnic sites; the provision or improvement of recreational parks; and the opening up of rights of way and National Trails.

The Countryside Commission recognises over 210 country parks and over 230 picnic sites in England. A further 24 country parks are recognised by the CCW. In Scotland there are 36 country parks, and the SNH has approved for grant aid many local authority and private sector schemes for a wide range of countryside facilities.

[4] For further information on the countryside in Britain see *Conservation* (Aspects of Britain: HMSO, 1993).

Total government funding of the countryside agencies in 1993–94 is over £40 million for the Countryside Commission, £19 million for the CCW and over £36 million for the SNH.

In Northern Ireland the Ulster Countryside Committee advises the Department of the Environment on the preservation of amenities and the designation of 'areas of outstanding natural beauty'.

The Sports Council works closely with the countryside agencies and supports their initiatives for open-air recreation. In 1992 the Council published a comprehensive policy statement on its countryside and water strategy, *A Countryside for Sport* (see Further Reading). The statement highlights the need for a strategic approach to the provision of facilities and for effective partnerships in addressing countryside issues.

## British Waterways Board

The British Waterways Board is a publicly owned body responsible for managing and developing much of Great Britain's inland waterways. Many leisure and recreational pursuits are enjoyed on waterways and reservoirs and in waterside buildings; these include angling, numerous types of sailing and boating, and specialist activities such as industrial archaeology. The Board, which is responsible for approximately 2,000 miles (3,220 km) of canals and water navigations, actively promotes water safety and organises community activities, such as canalside youth schemes.

## National Coaching Foundation

The National Coaching Foundation (NCF) was established in 1983 to provide educational and advisory services for coaches in all sports. The Foundation works in partnership with the Sports Councils, and its work complements and supports the coaching development carried out by sports governing bodies. Sixteen national coaching centres provide locally accessible services in coach education, information and advice as well as research and consultancy.

In 1991 the Sports Council published a major review of coaching in Britain, *Coaching Matters* (see Further Reading), which emphasised the role and importance of coaches and identified a better structure for their training and accreditation. The report recommended that the NCF should pursue the following priorities:

—the development of National Vocational Qualifications (NVQs) for coaches;[5]

—the setting up of a register of coaches;

—in-service training provision for coaches;

—local coaching development strategies;

—the production of guidelines for the employment of coaches; and

—raising the status of coaches and coaching.

The NCF's Coach Development Programme already provides a wide range of in-service courses for coaches, and a study has been commissioned into the possibility of producing a coaches' register. Local coaching strategies are examined in an advisory booklet.

In 1991–92 the Sports Council provided a grant of £700,000 to the NCF to enable it to set up Champion Coaching, a pilot after-school coaching scheme for those aged 11 to 14. The scheme led to

---

[5] For further information on NVQs see *Education* (Aspects of Britain: HMSO, 1993).

a number of high-quality coaching initiatives taking place in 24 areas in England involving over 6,000 youngsters. Following a £1.3 million grant from the Foundation for Sport and the Arts (see p. 43), the pilot scheme has been developed into a three-year programme, which will involve an estimated 40,000 children and some 4,000 coaches.

## British Olympic Association

The British Olympic Association (BOA), founded in 1905, is the National Olympic Committee for Britain and comprises representatives of the 31 governing bodies of those sports in the programme of the Olympic Games (summer and winter). Its primary function is to organise the participation of British teams in the Olympic Games, but it is also responsible for nominating British cities for staging the Olympics.

The BOA determines the size of British Olympic teams and sets standards for selection, raises funds, makes all arrangements and provides a headquarters staff for the management of the teams. It also makes important contributions in the fields of coaching, drug testing and control, and sports medicine. The Association's British Olympic Medical Centre at Northwick Park Hospital in north London supplies a medical back-up service for competitors before and during the Olympic Games.

The BOA encourages the involvement of sportsmen and women in policy-making and includes representatives from competitive sport on the National Olympic Committee, the policy-making body within the BOA. The BOA's Olympic Education Trust is concerned with educating young people and schoolchildren in fair play and the benefits of sport, encourages participation and teaches Olympic history.

The BOA is entirely self-supporting. Its funding is raised through sponsorship and by donations from commerce and industry and from the public.

## National Playing Fields Association

The National Playing Fields Association is a charity with a Royal Charter, whose purpose is to promote the provision of recreation and play facilities for all age groups. It aims to ensure that there are adequate playing fields and playspace available for use by the community. There are affiliated associations in the English and Welsh counties and independent organisations in Scotland and Northern Ireland.

A major study of England's recreational land was completed in October 1993 as part of a strategy to safeguard playing fields. The £500,000 project, funded by the Department of National Heritage, was commissioned by the Sports Council, the National Playing Fields Association and the CCPR. The Register of Recreational Land is the first ever comprehensive record of England's sports pitches and their facilities and took two years to complete. It reveals that England has over 73,000 pitches on some 24,000 sites, about half of which are owned by education authorities. The Register will play a key role in future sports planning and management and will be regularly updated.

There has been a substantial increase in recent years in the number of artificial turf pitches in Britain. Over 40 were developed in 1991–92, and there are now some 600 artificial pitches in England alone.

## Sports Medicine and Sports Science

Sports medicine and sports science are increasingly being acknowledged as important for assisting the improvement of performance and the achievement of excellence. In order to provide a more co-ordinated service to sportsmen and women, the Sports Council has established a National Sports Medicine Institute, based at St Bartholomew's Hospital, London.

The Institute has been incorporated as a limited company with charitable status and has on its Committee of Management representatives of all the Sports Councils, the BOA, the British Association of Sport and Medicine, the Chartered Society of Physiotherapy and the Royal Colleges of Surgeons and Physicians.

Facilities at the Institute include a physiology laboratory, accredited by the British Association of Sports Science (BASS), and a library and information centre. The Institute's main function is to provide clinical services aimed at assessing and improving fitness and treating and preventing medical disorders related to sport. However, it also provides training, carries out research and co-ordinates sports medicine activities. Work is in progress to develop a network of regional centres to provide both clinical and educational services, which will be linked with new support services at the National Sports Centres (see p. 27). The Sports Council is to allocate £500,000 towards sports medicine in 1993–94.

In Scotland a network of some 30 sports medicine centres has been created providing an effective system of primary care for sports injuries. In addition, the Scottish Sports Council's Consultative Group in Sports Medicine and Sports Sciences produces extensive educational material and holds regular seminars for doctors, physiotherapists and scientists.

An advisory service for sports governing bodies is provided by the British Association of Sport and Medicine, which organises courses in a variety of subjects. Higher education courses in sports medicine include a Master of Science course at Nottingham

University, established with the assistance of Sports Council funding, and a distance learning course at Bath University.

The development of sports science support services for the national governing bodies of sport is currently being promoted by the Sports Council, in collaboration with the BOA, the NCF and the BASS, in order to raise the standards of performance of national squads and to address the problems faced by elite performers. In 1993–94 the Sports Council will contribute £550,000 in support of science studies. It will also hold a number of workshops for governing bodies, coaches and sports scientists to encourage the use of sports science in governing body plans for performance and excellence. The Sports Council for Wales received £250,000 from the Welsh Office in 1992–93 to establish a Sports Science Centre in Wales.

## National Exercise and Fitness Association

Following the dramatic growth in the last ten years in the exercise and fitness industry, the Sports Council has proposed the establishment of a new governing body for England—the National Exercise and Fitness Association.

Although there are various organisations involved in providing membership services or training, there is no single body that the general public can contact for information on how to find good exercise classes and teachers or how to become qualified.

A working group representing a cross-section of the exercise and fitness industry was set up by the Sports Council in 1992 to prepare for the establishment of the national governing body. The Association would have six key aims:

—to provide information and advice to teachers and the public on exercise and fitness;

—to lead and co-ordinate the development of exercise and fitness in line with the needs and interests of its members and the public;

—to establish quality control and set standards for a competitive (amateur) structure for the sport;

—to liaise and work with the relevant bodies for the implementation of NVQ standards;

—to promote participation in exercise and fitness for all; and

—to help to secure good training and career development for exercise and fitness teachers.

Membership would be open to exercise and fitness teachers, competitors, trainers, coaches, and anyone interested in exercise and fitness.

# National Sports Centres

The four Sports Councils operate a total of 12 National Sports Centres, which provide world-class facilities for training and competition at the highest level. First priority at the Centres is given to the governing bodies of sport for national squad training and for the training of coaches. However, the Centres also make their facilities available to top sportsmen and women for individual training and to the local community. All of the Centres provide residential facilities.

## England

The Sports Council operates four major National Centres in England. Three of the Centres—Bisham Abbey (Berkshire), Crystal Palace (London) and Lilleshall (Shropshire)—have extensive specialist and multi-purpose indoor and outdoor facilities and are able to cater for a wide range of sports. Holme Pierrepont in Nottinghamshire is a specialist watersports centre, which offers, among other things, an artificially constructed training and competition facility for canoeing. The Sports Council also runs a minor National Centre for climbers at Harrison's Rocks near Groombridge in Kent. A sixth National Sports Centre—the National Cycling Centre—is due to open in Manchester in late 1994 (see p. 67).

### Crystal Palace
Crystal Palace is a leading competition venue for a wide range of sports and a major training centre for national squads, clubs,

schools and serious enthusiasts. Its facilities are used by 22 separate governing bodies of sport, including the Amateur Athletic Association, the Amateur Boxing Association and the British Judo Association, while the Centre is a regional centre of excellence for athletics, netball, weightlifting and swimming. The joint Crystal Palace/Amateur Swimming Association teaching scheme is the largest of its kind in Europe, making extensive use of the Centre's renowned swimming and diving facilities.

Crystal Palace stadium is Britain's major international athletics venue, with a capacity for 17,000 spectators. Other facilities include:

—an Olympic-size swimming pool;

—a 20-metre diving pool and separate teaching and training pools;

—four badminton courts and six squash courts;

—two general-purpose training halls;

—a boxing hall;

—a covered athletics training and warm-up area;

—fitness training and weightlifting facilities;

—an indoor five-a-side football area;

—four all-weather floodlit tennis/netball courts;

—two floodlit synthetic playing areas for football and hockey;

—an indoor climbing wall; and

—a dry-ski slope.

Coaching sessions for top sportsmen and women take place on a regular basis, as do training courses for teachers and coaches. There are also courses in a number of activities for individuals at a less advanced level who wish to improve their sporting skills or to learn the basics of a particular sport. Use of Crystal Palace's facilities is also extended to schoolchildren in the area, who are taught by qualified teachers in a range of indoor and outdoor sports.

The Crystal Palace Sports Injury Centre is one of the finest in Britain and is used by sportsmen and women at all levels of ability. The Centre provides the very latest equipment for treatment and rehabilitation and carries out research into sports injuries.

**Bisham Abbey**

Bisham Abbey was established in 1946 as Britain's first National Sports Centre. Today it caters for a wide range of sports, including tennis, football, hockey, weightlifting, squash, rugby and golf. The England football, rugby and hockey squads undergo regular preparation work at the Centre, together with Davis Cup tennis players and British international weightlifters.

Bisham Abbey has long-standing partnerships with the British Amateur Weightlifters Association and the Lawn Tennis Association (LTA), which has helped to develop the Abbey as the National Tennis Training Centre. The LTA runs a residential training school there, which is currently attended by seven boys and four girls between the ages of 12 and 16. National tennis squads are given extensive guaranteed periods of exclusive use of the indoor and outdoor courts.

The Centre has four indoor tennis courts and ten outdoor floodlit courts. Other facilities include:

—a floodlit synthetic football/hockey pitch;

—three grass football/rugby pitches;

—two squash courts;

—a nine-hole golf course;

—a weightlifting hall; and

—a sports injuries clinic.

The most recent development is the National Strength and Fitness Centre, which includes extensive aerobic and strength machines and a permanent Olympic weight-training base.

In addition to meeting the needs of the governing bodies of sport, the Centre makes its facilities available to the local community, and runs courses for beginners and school groups. Several non-residential tennis courses are run during the summer, and courses in sailing and canoeing take place on the nearby River Thames.

### Lilleshall

Lilleshall National Sports Centre offers extensive quality indoor and outdoor sports facilities, which are used by a variety of national teams. Facilities include a world-class gymnastic training centre, regularly used by the British gymnastic squads, and extensive playing fields for football and hockey. The Football Association (FA) uses Lilleshall as its base for major coaching activities and has established a residential two-year training school there for 14-year-old boys.

The Centre also offers training facilities for cricket, archery, table tennis, golf, volleyball, and billiards and snooker. A medical service is provided at the FA Rehabilitation and Sports Injury Clinic and the FA Human Performance Testing Unit, both of which are open to all sports competitors. Other facilities include:

— seven tennis courts;

— five squash courts;

— multi-purpose sports halls equipped for a variety of sports;

— an indoor archery centre;

— a bowls lawn; and

— an orienteering course.

Although the Centre is primarily for elite performers, such as Test cricketers and international football and hockey players, it is also widely used by the local community for activities such as special-interest weekends—a service which Lilleshall is seeking to expand.

### Holme Pierrepont

The National Watersports Centre at Holme Pierrepont in Nottinghamshire is one of the most comprehensive water sports centres in the world, with facilities for rowing, canoeing, water ski-ing, powerboating, ski-racing, angling and sailing. Holme Pierrepont's main features are a 2,000 m regatta course, a separate water ski lagoon and a new world-class canoe slalom course, which can cater for the needs of competitors of all ability levels.

The Centre has played an important role in the national train-ing and competitive programmes of the Amateur Rowing Association, the British Canoe Union, the British Water Ski Federation and the Royal Yachting Association. World Championship events take place at Holme Pierrepont every few years, and international tournaments are held regularly in various watersports. The British Canoe Union has recently taken up resi-dence at the Centre, and both the Oxford and Cambridge University Boat Clubs have used Holme Pierrepont for winter training.

The Centre offers a wide range of non-residential training courses for the novice and expert enthusiast, including a water sports summer programme for young people and special multi-activity courses for schools and clubs.

## Wales

There are three National Sports Centres in Wales. The Sports Council for Wales runs two: the Welsh Institute of Sport (formerly known as the National Sports Centre for Wales) in Cardiff and the National Watersports Centre at Plas Menai in north Wales. The other Centre—Plas y Brenin (north Wales)—is run by the Sports Council and specialises in mountain activities.

### The Welsh Institute of Sport

The Welsh Institute of Sport is the country's premier venue for top-level training and for competition in a large number of sports. The Centre plays a key role in supporting the overall development of sport in Wales and has some of the best indoor facilities in Britain. These include a world-standard, purpose-built gymnastics hall; a sports science unit and sports injury clinic; and a 25 m swimming pool with electronic timing. The Centre also has a number of all-weather tennis courts and floodlit artificial and grass pitches. As well as catering for the needs of the governing bodies of sport in Wales, the Institute runs a number of courses for sports clubs and schools. In 1991-92 a £1.25 million refurbishment was started.

### Plas Menai

The National Watersports Centre at Plas Menai is primarily a centre of excellence for sailing and canoeing, but also stages mountain activities in nearby Snowdonia. Its extensive range of activities include dinghy and catamaran sailing, offshore cruising and powerboat training. The Centre works closely with the Welsh Yachting and Canoe Associations, and their parent bodies, the Royal Yachting Association and the British Canoe Union. In recent years it has gained an international reputation as a leading centre in the development of training systems and safety routines. As well as catering for expert enthusiasts, Plas Menai offers a comprehensive range of courses for beginners and improvers.

## Plas y Brenin

Plas y Brenin National Mountain Centre is situated in Snowdonia National Park in north Wales. It offers a variety of courses in rock climbing, mountaineering, sea and river canoeing, orienteering, skiing and most other mountain-based activities. The courses cater for a wide range of abilities, from the beginner to the expert, and can be tailored to the needs of a particular group. Special courses are available for young people aged 13 to 16, the 50-plus age group, families, and women only. For 1992-93 the Council expanded its range of introductory courses in all activities so that more people learning the sport would have the opportunity of being taught the basic techniques and safety measures from well-qualified and experienced instructors.

The Centre co-operates closely with the governing bodies of mountaineering, canoeing, orienteering and skiing, and offers a wide range of courses in support of their national coaching and leadership schemes. Facilities at Plas y Brenin include a canoe training pool, a floodlit artificial ski slope, a heated indoor pool, an indoor climbing wall and a multi-gym. One of the Centre's most important users—the Mountain Leadership Training Board—has recently moved its offices to the Centre.

## Scotland

Scotland has three National Sports Centres, which are operated by the Scottish Sports Council: Glenmore Lodge National Outdoor Training Centre, near Aviemore; Inverclyde National Sports Training Centre, at Largs; and Cumbrae National Water Sports Training Centre on the island of Great Cumbrae in the Firth of Clyde.

### Glenmore Lodge

The National Outdoor Training Centre at Glenmore Lodge caters for a wide range of both summer and winter activities, including hill walking, rock climbing, mountaineering, kayaking, skiing and canoeing. Its facilities include an indoor climbing wall, a dry ski slope, two artificial rock-climbing towers and a large canoe pond with slalom gates. The Centre is currently undergoing a £1.6 million redevelopment programme with the help of an £800,000 government grant. In 1992 the Centre played a key role in establishing the new European Mountain Leader Award.

### Inverclyde

The Inverclyde National Sports Training Centre has a wide range of facilities, including a gymnastics hall, floodlit tennis and netball courts, a purpose-built golf training facility and a Human Performance Laboratory for fitness assessment. As well as serving the needs of the governing bodies of sport, the Centre has an extensive sports programme for local clubs and other enthusiasts. The Centre also acts as an important competition venue for major national and international championships. In 1992 these included the Scottish Open Table Tennis Championship and the World Youth Sailing Championship.

### Cumbrae

The Cumbrae National Water Sports Training Centre offers an extensive range of courses catering for all levels of ability. The Centre has a comprehensive range of modern craft for a wide variety of sailing activities, as well as various sea canoes and sub-aqua diving equipment. In addition to its full programme of race training, instructor courses and courses for the general public, major events are staged every year, including in 1992 the British Junior National Sailing Championship. A permanent staff of Royal Yachting Association coaches and instructors provides expert training.

## Northern Ireland

The Sports Council for Northern Ireland runs one national facility—the Northern Ireland Centre for Outdoor Activities—at Tollymore in County Down.

### Tollymore

The Northern Ireland Centre for Outdoor Activities offers courses in mountaineering, rock climbing, canoeing and outdoor adventure. Also available are leadership and instructor courses leading to nationally recognised qualifications in mountain leader training, canoe instructor training, rock climbing and adventure activities. The courses mostly take place at weekends, with some longer courses in other parts of Great Britain and Ireland and in the Alps.

# Sport for People with Disabilities

## Associations for People with Disabilities

Opportunities exist for people with disabilities to take part in a variety of sporting activities. The key organisations are the British Sports Association for the Disabled, the United Kingdom Sports Association for People with Learning Disability, the British Paralympic Association and a range of bodies concerned with individual disabilities and single sports. These include the Riding for the Disabled Association, which caters for some 25,000 riders, and the British Disabled Water Ski Association, which offers training and competition to a growing number of skiers.

### British Sports Association for the Disabled

The British Sports Association for the Disabled (BSAD) is a national body working across all the disabilities. It promotes the development of sport at local level for people with disabilities, and organises regional and national championships in a range of sports. The BSAD has a membership of over 500 clubs, colleges and schools, with around 50,000 individual members. As well as providing information and advice to local clubs and groups, it arranges a number of conferences, seminars and coaching courses. The BSAD also maintains close contact with local authorities and the regional offices of the Sports Council. It aims to employ at least one development officer in each of the Sports Council's ten regions in England.

The Scottish Sports Association for the Disabled, the Federation of Sports Associations for the Disabled (Wales) and the Northern Ireland Committee on Sport for Disabled People have similar co-ordinating roles.

## United Kingdom Sports Association for People with Learning Disability

The United Kingdom Sports Association for People with Learning Disability is a co-ordinating body with a membership of over 20 national organisations. The Association was set up in 1980 and is active at local, national and international level promoting and supporting the work of its members and providing training. It works closely with the British Paralympic Association in co-ordinating the participation of people with learning difficulties in the Paralympics (see p. 65).

## National Disability Sports Organisations

There are six national disability sports organisations concerned with individual disabilities. These organisations provide coaching at local, national and international level and help to organise national competitions in conjunction with the national governing bodies of sport and the BSAD. They comprise:

—the British Amputee Sports Association;

—British Blind Sport;

—the British Deaf Sports Council;

—the British Wheelchair Sports Foundation;

—Cerebral Palsy Sport; and

—the British Les Autres Sports Association, which was formed in 1982 to cater for those whose different disabilities are not covered by other organisations.

# The Paralympic Games

The Paralympic Games are the world's most important event for people with disabilities. Held every four years, the Paralympics encompass a wide range of sports and attract competitors from around the world. Events in the Paralympics are divided into a number of different categories so that participants can compete with others of a similar disability.

Evolving from the Stoke Mandeville Games held to coincide with the 1948 Olympic Games, the Paralympics were first held in Rome in 1960 and attracted some 400 athletes from 23 countries. In Seoul in 1988 the Olympics and Paralympics shared the same venues, with the Paralympics taking place one month after the able-bodied Games. This arrangement was repeated in Barcelona in 1992, with the added provision of accommodation in the Olympic Village for the first time as a result of the organising committee of the Olympics being also responsible for the organisation of the Paralympics.

Britain's participation in the Paralympics is organised by the British Paralympic Association (BPA), which liaises closely with the British Olympic Association. The BPA takes a lead role in the preparation and training of Paralympic and other international teams, and advises the Sports Council on the distribution of grants for all international disabled sports events.

The first-ever Paralympic Games for people with learning difficulties were held in Madrid in September 1992 (see p. 65), immediately after the Paralympics for people with physical disabilities.

# Government Report

In 1989 the Government published a report on sport for people with disabilities—*Building on Ability* (see Further Reading). This recommended that sport for disabled and able-bodied people should be increasingly integrated, with athletes with disabilities being encouraged to participate in sporting events either in direct competition with able-bodied athletes or in parallel events. It also recommended that governing bodies of sport should increasingly assume responsibility for all participants in their sport, whether able-bodied or disabled.

The report said that the Sports Council should take into account in all its activities the needs of disabled people and should establish a standing conference on sport for people with disabilities. Additional funds should be provided by the Council to assist disability sports organisations, and the National Sports Centres should draw up a strategy for encouraging more disabled athletes to use their facilities. Governing bodies should be required by the Sports Council to prepare a strategy for sport for people with disabilities and include this in the plans they submit when applying for financial aid.

Local authorities, the report recommended, should assume responsibility for ensuring provision and co-ordination of sport at local level for people with disabilities. They should be fully aware of the voluntary organisations promoting sport in their area and should seek to assist them through financial and other means. Local authorities should work with the private and voluntary sectors to make sure that all sports facilities are accessible to disabled people.

## Response to the Report

Following publication of the report, the Government provided the BPA with £500,000 for the establishment of a trust fund to support a variety of disabled sport initiatives. In 1991 the Government contributed an additional £300,000 to the Sports Council and £35,000 to the Scottish Sports Council to help implement the report's recommendations. Substantial grants have also been made by the Foundation for Sport and the Arts to assist sporting activities by people with disabilities.

The governing bodies of sport are increasingly taking responsibility for both able-bodied participants and those with disabilities. Close liaison takes place between individual sports and the Sports Council, which provides advice to governing bodies on the production of strategies for encouraging the integration of people with disabilities. In 1991–92 specific work was undertaken with 23 governing bodies on schemes to promote integration. The first disability forum was held by the Sports Council in December 1991 to discuss issues of common concern and to provide advice to disability sports organisations.

## Additional Funding

In 1993 the Sports Council agreed to give additional financial support to sport for people with  disabilities through the fund-raising activities of the National Swimathon. The Swimathon is a marathon swimming event, which involves individuals and teams of all levels of ability swimming 5,000 metres in aid of charity. In 1993 some 35,000 swimmers took part in over 300 pools throughout Britain. Approximately £1.5 million was raised for charity, 10 per cent of which was donated towards the development of sport at grass roots level for people with disabilities. This donation was matched by the Sports Council.

The money is to be used by the British Sports Association for the Disabled and the United Kingdom Sports Association for People with Learning Disability to extend their range of provision and to undertake a range of regional training initiatives with local authority staff, volunteers and sports coaches.

# Sponsorship and Other Funding

The private sector makes a substantial investment in sports sponsorship, contributing some £230 million a year. This involves more than 2,000 British companies, and investment ranges from support for Britain's efforts in the Olympic Games to sport at the local level.

Sponsorship may take the form of financing specific events, or of grants to individual sports organisations or sportsmen and women. Investment includes sponsorship of cricket and football leagues, sporting events such as horse races, and of individual performers. Motor sport and football receive the largest amounts of private sponsorship.

Sponsorship of sport is encouraged by a number of bodies, including the Institute of Sports Sponsorship (ISS—see p. 17), the Scottish Sports Council's Sponsorship Advisory Service, which has raised almost £3 million directly for Scottish sport over the last ten years, and the Sports Council for Wales' Sponsorship Advisory Service, which in its first two years of operation has helped generate £140,000 for Welsh sport.

Successive governments have negotiated voluntary agreements with the tobacco industry to regulate tobacco companies' sponsorship of sport, the last one having come into force in 1987. This has the aim of promoting responsible sponsorship activities and imposes a ceiling on spending by tobacco firms on sports sponsorship. It prohibits sponsorship of events where a majority of the participants are under 18 years of age or which are designed to appeal mainly to spectators under 18. It bans the depiction of any participants in a sport in media advertising, and imposes strict controls on siting of signs at televised events and on the size of health warnings on these signs.

## Business Sponsorship Scheme

In an effort to increase the current levels of sports sponsorship, the Government has established a business sponsorship incentive scheme for sport similar to that run for the arts and targeted at the 'grass roots' level. The `Sportsmatch' scheme was launched at the end of 1992 and assists local sport by providing government funds to match those from business sponsors. Sportsmatch will provide funding of over £3.7 million a year in Great Britain to match funds from the private sector.

In England the scheme is managed as a joint venture between the Department of National Heritage and the ISS. Under the scheme, local sport can gain up to £75,000 a project from the Government if the same amount is secured in business sponsorship. Sportsmatch intends to concentrate on local amateur sport and to encourage firms which have not used sponsorship before as part of their promotional activities.

The Government has emphasised that the scheme is aimed at developing sport at a local level and will not include national professional sports initiatives. The Sportsmatch Awards Panel, which meets regularly to consider the distribution of grants, is looking in particular for schemes in inner cities and rural areas lacking sporting resources. It is also especially interested in sporting projects targeted at the young, disabled people and ethnic minorities. To qualify for an award, an event or activity must be competitive, challenging and involve some physical skill. The sport must be amateur, but the Panel would not exclude the payment of professional sportsmen and women to coach amateurs.

The first awards ranged from £1,000 to help a sports club and a local school to form a closer partnership to £75,000 for a new sports facility which will provide gymnastics and other sporting opportunities for children.

Similar arrangements have been announced for the new scheme in Scotland and Wales, where it will be administered by the Scottish Sports Council and the Sports Council for Wales in association with the ISS. Northern Ireland has its own sports sponsorship incentive scheme, which is currently being reviewed.

## Sports Aid Foundation

The Sports Aid Foundation (SAF) assists the training of talented individuals by raising and distributing funds from industry, commerce and private sponsors. Grants are awarded on the recommendation of the appropriate governing bodies of sport to British competitors who need help preparing for Olympic, World and European championships. The Scottish and Welsh Sports Aid Foundations and the Ulster Sports and Recreation Trust have similar functions. The SAF is an independent organisation which is entirely self-funding.

Through the Sports Aid Foundation Charitable Trust, a registered charity, grants are awarded to talented sportsmen and women who are in education or on a low income and to competitors with disabilities to help them develop their sporting potential.

## Foundation for Sport and the Arts

The Foundation for Sport and the Arts was set up by the pools promoters in 1991 to channel funds into sport and the arts. The pools promoters are providing the Foundation with some £43.5 million a year. A further £21.8 million a year is received as a result of the 2.5 per cent reduction in pool betting duty in the 1991 Budget. About £43.5 million a year is available for sport.

The Foundation works closely with the Sports Councils and other sports bodies, and makes numerous grants to sports clubs and sporting organisations. Its main aims are to support the improvement of existing facilities, to assist the construction of new sports venues, and to help as wide a variety of projects as possible.

The Foundation has provided substantial sums of money for sport in schools, sport for people with disabilities, and the British Olympic and Paralympic teams.

Recent assistance includes:

—a contribution of £1 million towards the proposed Northern Ireland Sports Training Centre at Queen's University, Belfast;

—a sum of £50,000 for the development of training facilities at the Alexandra Palace Ice Rink in north London;

—a grant of £100,000 to Widnes Rugby League FC to assist with the upgrading of facilities at the ground to comply with the recommendations of the Taylor Report (see p. 54);

—£200,000 to Yorkshire & Cleveland Riding for the Disabled to assist with the cost of providing a major centre for disabled riders;

—a sum of £30,000 to Wrexham Maelor Borough Council to construct a fourth indoor tennis court at the North Wales Regional Tennis Centre;

—£17,500 to Dungannon Basketball Club to help the club conduct a cross-community basketball programme for children throughout a large area of the province; and

—a grant of £10,000 to the Scottish Cricket Union to assist the funding of the cricket tour of South Africa in 1993.

# Horserace Betting Levy

Most betting in Britain takes place on horse racing and greyhound racing. Bets may be made at racecourses and greyhound tracks, or through over 10,000 licensed off-course betting offices, which take about 90 per cent of the money staked. Licensed betting offices were permitted to open in the evening for the first time in summer 1993 so that they could take advantage of evening race meetings.

A form of pool betting—totalisator betting—is organised on racecourses by the Horserace Totalisator Board (the Tote), whose members are appointed by the Home Secretary. Racecourse bets may also be placed with independent on-course bookmakers.

Bookmakers and the Tote contribute a levy—a fixed proportion of their profits—to the Horserace Betting Levy Board. The amount of levy payable is decided by the racing and bookmaking industries, but the Home Secretary can be called upon to intervene if agreement between the two sides cannot be reached.

The Levy Board promotes the improvement of horse breeds, advancement of veterinary science and better horse racing. Its funding activities include loan funding of racecourse improvements, an annual contribution towards the training of stable and stud staff, and the regular sponsorship of races. The Levy Board's contribution to prize money for 1994 is set to rise by £1.2 million to £27 million.

In 1991–92 the total money staked in all forms of gambling, excluding gaming machines, was estimated at £24,594 million.

# National Lottery

In March 1992 the Government set out its proposals for a new national lottery in a White Paper—*A National Lottery Raising*

*Money for Good Causes* (see Further Reading). This recommended that sport should be one of the main beneficiaries of such a lottery, which could be in operation by late 1994. Following publication of the White Paper, the Government sought views on various aspects of the proposed lottery, including its nature and frequency, and the effect on football pools and other forms of gambling.

The main provisions of the National Lottery etc. Act 1993, which paves the way for the introduction of the new National Lottery, are that:

—the Lottery should be run by the private sector and be regulated by a Director General of the National Lottery;

—the Director General will issue one main licence for running the Lottery, and a series of sub-licences for individual games; and

—a National Lottery Distribution Fund will be established, with the proceeds being divided equally between arts, sports, the national heritage, charities, and projects to mark the year 2000 and the beginning of the third millennium (the Millennium Fund).

It is likely that the maximum price of a ticket would be no more than £1.

The Government recognises that the pools industry will be affected by the National Lottery, but believes that the effect will not be significant, as the Lottery is expected to attract those who do not usually take part in the pools or other forms of gambling. In other countries it has been found that lotteries do not, in general, appeal to serious gamblers but attract those who like to know that, should they lose, the money spent will go to good causes. The Government intends to set a minimum age of 16 for those who can buy or sell tickets.

Sport will qualify for 20 per cent of the available proceeds from the Lottery, as will each of the other four categories (see p. 46). However, these proportions could be amended, and the Government intends to review the allocation once during each Parliament. With the exception of the Millennium Fund, each of the five qualifying categories will have to receive at least 5 per cent of the proceeds. The Government expects the distributors of the proceeds to concentrate on projects that would not normally receive first call on public expenditure.

The money for sport will be split between the four Sports Councils. Once fully operational, the National Lottery could raise up to £1,500 million a year.

# Sport and Education

All schools (except those solely for infants) are expected to have a playing field or the use of one, and most secondary schools have a gymnasium. Some have other amenities such as swimming pools, sports halls and halls designed for dance and movement.

## National Curriculum

The Government believes that all young children should have the opportunity to learn basic sports skills. It has therefore made physical education (PE), which includes sport, a compulsory subject in the National Curriculum for all pupils aged 5 to 16 in state-maintained schools in England and Wales. Schools will need to ensure that sufficient time is devoted to PE to enable the requirements to be met.

The PE National Curriculum states that during key stages 1 and 2 (ages 5 to 11) pupils are required to pursue programmes of study for five areas of activity: athletic activities, dance, games, gymnastic activities, and outdoor and adventurous activities. They are also required to cover from autumn 1994 a programme of study for swimming and to have been taught to swim at least 25 metres unaided by the end of key stage 2.

In key stage 3 (ages 11 to 14) pupils are required to pursue a minimum of four areas of activity. One of the activities in each year must be games, with at least three further areas of activity from athletic activities, dance, gymnastic activities, and outdoor and adventurous activities to be undertaken at some point during the key stage.

In key stage 4 (ages 14 to 16) pupils not taking GCSE (General Certificate of Secondary Education) in PE, dance or any other related area should study at least two activities. These may be drawn from the same area of activity (for example, football and cricket—both games) or from two different areas (for example, athletics and dance).

Pupils who wish to pursue swimming and other water-based activities at key stages 3 and 4 are allowed to do so where schools have appropriate facilities: for example, swimming as an athletic activity, water polo as a game, or canoeing as an outdoor and adventurous activity.

For the first-year pupils of key stages 1 to 3 these requirements came into effect from August 1992, with the provisions coming into force for the others in these age groups at yearly intervals from August 1993. The provisions come into force for key stage 4 pupils from August 1995.

There is no statutory national curriculum in Scotland. However, National Guidelines on each curricular area are issued by the Secretary of State for Scotland for implementation by education authorities and schools. The National Guidelines on Expressive Arts (which includes physical education) contain programmes of study and attainment targets for games, team sports, dance, gymnastics, athletics, swimming and outdoor education for each of five levels covering pupils aged 5 to 14.

## Other Sports Activities in Schools

The Government is to issue guidance to schools to suggest the sort of information that they should make readily available to parents, possibly by publication in school prospectuses. Schools will be encouraged to provide details of their sports facilities, the range of opportunities for sporting activities, details of their sporting links with the local community, as well as the success of school teams and pupils in local, regional and national sport.

A number of schools run proficiency schemes for their pupils in certain sports. In athletics, for example, there are a number of schemes which help to bridge the gap between school and sports club. These include the Five-Star Award Proficiency Scheme, operated by the Amateur Athletic Association in schools in England and Wales and the Amateur Athletic Federation in Northern Ireland, and the Young Athletes League. The Thistle Scheme in Scotland provides a similar type of proficiency scheme which enables young athletes to measure their own progress.

## Partnerships with the Local Community

The Government is encouraging stronger links between schools and the wider community to ensure that children have access to the sports amenities which clubs and associations can make available outside school hours. The Government's recent sports policy statement recorded a number of ways of promoting partnerships between schools and other organisations in the local community. The statement recommended:

—the nomination by every school of a teacher from existing staff who would have responsibility for developing awareness and use of community facilities by their pupils;

—the creation of opportunities within schools and colleges for pupils and students to organise and run their own sports clubs;

—the co-ordination by an appropriate local body, normally a local authority, of organisations involved in providing sport and active recreation for young people, including schools, colleges, sports clubs, the youth service and local employers; and

—the appointment of sports development officers by local authorities and sports governing bodies to promote sports links between schools, colleges and the community.

In Scotland an initiative aimed at strengthening the links between schools, clubs and the community was launched by the Scottish Sports Council in May 1991. 'Team Sport Scotland' seeks to promote the development of school-aged team sport and was made possible through a Scottish Office grant of £400,000 in the first year, with a commitment to further funding for the following two years. The initiative supports the setting up of clubs, particularly junior sections, and encourages the uptake of coaching courses by teachers, club leaders and parents. It also aims to develop partnership projects with local authorities and the private sector.

The team sports covered by the project are football, hockey, rugby, cricket, netball, basketball, volleyball and shinty (a Highland variation of hockey). A co-ordinator for each sport works closely with the relevant governing body, local authorities, local schools and other interested parties to foster and develop team sport by bringing together all the resources in the community. Each year Team Sport Scotland intends to hold one national and nine regional sports festivals, where children will have the opportunity to play organised matches and receive coaching sessions. The first national festival took place at Perth in May 1992 and attracted over 1,500 children from across Scotland.

## Community Use of School Facilities

To achieve the maximum use of sports facilities, the Government is encouraging greater community use of sports halls, playing fields and other facilities owned by schools and colleges. In October 1991 the Government launched a guide—*A Sporting Double: School and*

*Community* (see Further Reading)—to encourage and assist the sharing of school facilities between schools and the local community.

The guide provides practical guidance for teachers, governors and community groups to help them open up schools for a variety of sporting uses. The Government believes that the sharing of facilities provides a useful source of revenue for schools and can lead to a closer link between schools and the local community. The guide provides detailed information on how to arrange community use and on the benefits which can result. The Education Act 1993 includes provisions to allow school governors to enter into agreements for the joint management of school premises for community purposes.

## Play and Recreation for Children

The Department of National Heritage co-ordinates policy on children's play in England and issues guidance on playground safety. Following the closure of the National Children's Play and Recreation Unit in March 1993, the Sports Council has taken over the National Play Information Centre and the Unit's responsibilities for playwork education and training. In addition, the Sports Council's Trust Company has provided a grant to the National Voluntary Council for Children's Play.

In October 1992 the Sports Council announced the publication of a new resource pack for primary school teachers, produced in conjunction with the National Coaching Foundation and the British Council of Physical Education. The pack—*Teaching Children to Play Games*—provides up-to-date information on the skills which young people need to play sport and contains advice for teachers on various matters, such as dealing with large numbers of pupils and with groups of varying ability. The pack provides a wide range of teaching materials and recommends that teachers should encourage children to develop basic recreational skills and to avoid specialising too early in sport.

# Spectator Safety at Sports Grounds

Safety at sports grounds is governed by legislation. The main instrument of control is a safety certificate which is issued by the relevant local authority. When determining the conditions of a safety certificate, the local authority is expected to comply with the *Guide to Safety at Sports Grounds*. This was revised in 1990 to include the relevant safety recommendations of the 'Taylor Report' on the Hillsborough stadium disaster in Sheffield in 1989, which resulted in the death of 96 spectators.

## The Taylor Report

The Taylor Report, published in 1990 (see Further Reading), contained a wide range of recommendations for promoting better and safer conditions at all sports grounds.

The report examined in particular the current state of football and found that the game was suffering as a result of old grounds, poor facilities, lack of crowd control, and poor leadership on the part of the football authorities and the clubs. It considered that crowd safety and crowd behaviour were closely related to the quality of the accommodation and facilities in the stadiums and that provision made by football clubs for fans was often inadequate. Spectator behaviour could be improved not only by providing better physical conditions but also if all those involved in football—players, referees, managers and club directors—set a better example.

The report suggested ways of improving stadiums to provide spectators with modern facilities and recommended that most of the improvements to football grounds should be paid for by League clubs, using the many sources of revenue available to them, such as sponsorship and the sale of television rights for broadcasting matches. Among the report's recommendations were that:

—sports grounds designated under the Safety of Sports Grounds Act 1975 should become all-seated under a phased programme;

—standing capacity should be reduced during the phasing in of all-seated accommodation;

—the Football Association and the Football League should set up an Advisory Design Council to conduct research and to disseminate information and expertise regularly to League clubs;

—a National Inspectorate and Review Body should be set up to assess the way that local authorities certify sports grounds;

—perimeter fencing should be lowered and eventually removed altogether;

—all emergency exit gates in perimeter fences should be painted in distinctive colours and be kept unlocked during matches;

—clubs should recruit an adequate number of competent stewards;

—the police should be allocated proper control rooms and should be urged to review their operational orders for policing matches and their training for senior officers in charge of matches; and

—it should be made illegal to throw missiles or chant obscene or racist abuse in sports grounds.

The Government accepted most of the report's recommendations for making sports stadiums safer and agreed the timetables for the introduction of all-seater stadiums for football (see p. 56). It confirmed that all the necessary steps would be taken to ensure crowd control and better training for police and stewards. Under the Football Spectators Act 1989 the Government established a Football Licensing Authority (FLA), which is responsible for assisting in the implementation of the all-seating policy in England and Wales. The FLA operates a licensing system for grounds on which designated football matches are played and keeps under scrutiny the way in which local authorities carry out their safety functions under the Safety of Sports Grounds Act 1975. The first licences were issued by the FLA before the start of the 1993–94 football season.

## Football Grounds

In 1992 the Government reviewed its policy on requiring all League football grounds to have seated accommodation only. Clubs in the Premier League, First Division clubs in the Football League and national stadiums are still required to have all-seated accommodation by August 1994. However, this requirement has been relaxed for the Second and Third Divisions of the Football League, provided that the terracing is safe. Clubs moving from the Second to the First Division would continue to have three seasons to convert to all-seating accommodation. In Scotland Premier Division clubs and national stadiums must meet the 1994 deadline, but First and Second Division clubs may retain the use of standing accommodation.

## The Football Trust

The Football Trust 1990 was established by the pool promoters and replaced the Football Grounds Improvement Trust and the

The London Marathon, held annually in April, regularly attracts over 25,000 participants.

A group of children improvising a game of hockey in a primary school playground in Manchester.

Snowdonia National Park forms a spectacular backdrop to yachting at Pwllheli in north Wales.

The field for the Ascot Gold Cup passes in front of packed stands on Ladies Day at Royal Ascot.

England won the Women's World Cup for the second time in 1993, defeating New Zealand in the final.

Nick Gillingham winning the 200 metres breaststroke for the third time at the 1993 European Championships in Sheffield. He subsequently won the short-course version of the event at the 1993 world championships in Palma de Mallorca.

The Scottish National Sports Centre at Glenmore Lodge near Aviemore offers a wide range of courses in mountaineering and other outdoor activities.

Terry Hopkins – winner of a gold and a silver medal at the 1992 Paralympics in Barcelona.

Nigel Short playing against Gary Kasparov in the 1993 world chess championship at the Savoy Theatre in London.

earlier Football Trust. Its income is over £32 million a year. It is funded partly by the pool promoters from their spotting-the-ball competition and partly from a 2.5 per cent reduction in pool betting duty to run for five years, announced in the 1991 Budget. This concession will provide more than £100 million to football on the understanding that the money made available must be used to assist football clubs and the national stadiums to fund capital works for the comfort and safety of spectators and, in particular, all-seater stadiums in line with the recommendations of the Taylor Report.

In August 1993 the Government agreed to extend the concession for a further five years in order to help clubs in the lower divisions of the Football League to ensure that any terracing retained at their grounds meets the required safety standards. Spotting-the-ball funds are used for safety grants and projects such as closed-circuit television, contributions to police and stewarding costs at football grounds, and community football projects.

The Football Trust recently announced plans to establish a nationwide Grass Roots Facilities Scheme. Under the scheme, grants would be available for the provision of pitch and changing-room facilities on sites owned by local authorities, non-League clubs, schools, voluntary bodies and other organisations. A budget of over £1 million has been allocated to the scheme, which will be operated on a regional basis in consultation with the Sports Councils, football associations, local authorities and other interested parties.

## Crowd Control

Spectator violence associated with football both in Britain and overseas has been a subject of widespread concern, although there are signs that in recent years government policy and action have resulted in a decline in violence. The Government has worked closely with the police, football authorities and the governments of other European countries to implement measures to combat the problem. Within the Council of Europe, Britain contributes to the work of the Standing Committee on the European Convention on Spectator Violence. Britain was the first country to sign and ratify the Convention. It has welcomed the Committee's recommendation urging tough action against hooliganism, including prosecution where appropriate.

Recognising the link between excessive alcohol consumption and crowd disorder, the Government introduced legislation in Scotland in 1980 and in the rest of Britain in 1985 to establish controls on the sale and possession of alcohol at football grounds and on transport to and from grounds. Legislation has made it an offence in England and Wales to throw objects at football matches, run onto the playing area without good reason or chant indecent or racist abuse.

Courts in England and Wales have the power to prohibit convicted football hooligans from attending football matches. They also have powers to impose restriction orders on convicted football hooligans to prevent them travelling abroad to attend specified matches. Closed-circuit television has greatly assisted the police in controlling crowds and is an important evidence-gathering tool. The National Criminal Intelligence Service Football Unit co-ordinates police intelligence about football hooligans and strengthens liaison with overseas police forces.

# Drug Abuse in Sport

The use of drugs to improve athletic performance has been universally condemned by authorities, since the use of such drugs not only creates an unfair advantage but also endangers the health of those taking them. Random urine tests to detect abuse are carried out in most sports both in and out of competition. The two main types of drugs that are abused by sportsmen and women to enhance their performance are stimulants and anabolic steroids.

Stimulants are often taken to prevent fatigue and to increase self-confidence. However, they may also cause excessive aggression, which increases the risk of injury, and overuse may lead to heart disorders. Anabolic steroids are used to accelerate the recovery of muscles after strenuous exercise. This allows the taker to undergo a more exacting training schedule and causes an increase in muscle bulk and strength. Abuse of anabolic steroids is mostly found in sports which are based on physical strength, such as weightlifting and athletics (especially in field events and sprints). Prolonged use of anabolic steroids may cause liver damage and infertility.

## National Action

Drug-taking in sport to improve performance has been a cause of concern to the Government, the Sports Councils and the governing bodies of sport. Following a ministerial review, the Sports Council introduced a new independent drug-testing regime in 1988. This provides for random testing in and out of competition by independent sampling officers, and the publication of adverse findings.

The Sports Council provides financial support for the British drug-testing programme. It also funds the International Olympic Committee (IOC)-accredited laboratory at King's College, London University, which carries out analysis and research into methods of detection for new drugs which unfairly aid performance.

The Government is currently considering the possibility of strengthening legal controls on anabolic steroids. These are currently prescription-only medicines under the Medicines Act 1968.

### Recent Action

In 1992–93 the Sports Council intensified its drugs-testing programme. Greater emphasis was placed on out-of-competition tests, with the number rising to 747 in 1992–93, compared with 622 in 1991–92. From a total of over 4,150 samples taken both in and out of competition in 1992–93, there were 48 positive reports, compared with 53 the previous year. The number of athletes refusing to give samples fell from 22 to 10.

Sports Council funding in Britain for the programme exceeded £820,000 in 1992–93, part of which was spent on education and the dissemination of information. In 1993–94 the Council is to spend £100,000 on this aspect of the programme.

In 1991–92 The Scottish Office made an additional £50,000 available to the Scottish Sports Council to help in its programme against drug abuse in sport. Action by the Council included the launch in November 1992 of an Anti-doping Education Campaign at Meadowbank Stadium. The Campaign was one of the events which took place during European Drug Prevention Week.

## International Action

The Government and the Sports Council have taken action against drug misuse at international level. In 1990 the Council of Europe developed an Anti-Doping Convention to tackle the problem of drug abuse in sport. This was a British initiative, the main aims of which are to provide an international framework within which national anti-doping campaigns can work effectively. The convention seeks to:

—reinforce the ban on the use of drugs and doping methods as specified by the IOC;

—require signatory states to adopt legal and other measures to restrict the availability of prohibited drugs;

—ensure that grants are given only to those sports bodies with anti-doping regulations; and

—ensure that financial assistance is available to set up controls.

Signatory states are encouraged to set up doping-control laboratories meeting IOC standards, and sports governing bodies are urged to harmonise out-of-competition testing and other anti-doping regulations with those of the IOC. Testing at international events and out-of-competition testing by international sports bodies are also promoted under the new agreement. Britain has already implemented its provisions.

The Government has also signed anti-doping monitoring agreements with Australia, Canada and Norway, which provide for the mutual testing of athletes, both in and out of competition, and for mutual assessment of each other's testing systems.

## World Conference on Anti-doping in Sport

The Fourth Permanent World Conference on Anti-doping in Sport took place in London in September 1993. The Conference was organised by the Sports Council in association with the IOC Medical Commission and brought together more than 200 experts on drugs in sport from 60 countries. Delegates included scientists, doctors, coaches, sports administrators, government officials and representatives from international sports federations and the IOC. The three-day conference examined current anti-doping developments throughout the world, why competitors take drugs and how they obtain them, and the views of the next generation of competitors on drug abuse.

# International Sport

## Barcelona Olympics

More than 10,000 competitors from a record 172 countries took part in the 25th Modern Olympics at Barcelona in 1992. The British team won 20 medals—5 gold, 3 silver and 12 bronze—and finished in 13th position in the overall medals table, which was headed by the Unified Team (republics of the former Soviet Union) and the United States.

The number of medals won by Britain was four fewer than in the Seoul Olympics in 1988, although the number of gold medals was the same as in 1988 and in the previous two Olympics (see Table 2). The five gold medals were in athletics (two), rowing (two) and cycling. In athletics Sally Gunnell became the first British woman to win an Olympic track gold medal since 1964, and Linford Christie became the oldest ever winner of the 100 metres, at the age of 32. Chris Boardman's victory in the individual pursuit was Britain's first gold medal in cycling since 1920, and in rowing Steven Redgrave won his third consecutive Olympic gold medal.

### Gold Medals

*Athletics*: men's 100 metres—Linford Christie; women's 400 metres hurdles—Sally Gunnell.
*Cycling*: men's 4,000 metres individual pursuit—Chris Boardman.
*Rowing*: men's coxless pairs—Steven Redgrave and Matthew Pinsent; men's coxed pairs—Gregory Searle, Jonathan Searle and Garry Herbert (cox).

### Silver Medals

*Canoeing*: men's Canadian singles slalom——Gareth Marriott.

*Judo*: men's half-heavyweight (95 kg)—Ray Stevens; women's lightweight (56 kg)—Nicola Fairbrother.

**Bronze Medals**

*Archery*: men's 70 metres individual—Simon Terry; team—Steven Hallard, Richard Priestman and Simon Terry.

*Athletics*: men's 400 metres hurdles—Kriss Akabusi; men's javelin—Steve Backley; men's 4 x 400 metres relay—Roger Black, David Grindley, Kriss Akabusi and John Regis; women's 4 x 400 metres relay—Phyliss Smith, Sandra Douglas, Jenny Stoute and Sally Gunnell.

*Boxing*: light middleweight: Robin Reid.

*Hockey*: women's team.

*Judo*: women's middleweight (66 kg)—Kate Howey; women's half-lightweight (52 kg)—Sharon Rendle.

**Table 2:  Olympic Medals won by Britain since 1948**

|      |             | Gold | Silver | Bronze | Total |
|------|-------------|------|--------|--------|-------|
| 1948 | London      | 3    | 14     | 6      | 23    |
| 1952 | Helsinki    | 1    | 2      | 8      | 11    |
| 1956 | Melbourne   | 6    | 7      | 11     | 24    |
| 1960 | Rome        | 2    | 6      | 12     | 20    |
| 1964 | Tokyo       | 4    | 12     | 2      | 18    |
| 1968 | Mexico City | 5    | 5      | 3      | 13    |
| 1972 | Munich      | 4    | 5      | 9      | 18    |
| 1976 | Montreal    | 3    | 5      | 5      | 13    |
| 1980 | Moscow      | 5    | 7      | 9      | 21    |
| 1984 | Los Angeles | 5    | 11     | 21     | 37    |
| 1988 | Seoul       | 5    | 10     | 9      | 24    |
| 1992 | Barcelona   | 5    | 3      | 12     | 20    |

*Swimming*: men's 200 metres breaststroke—Nick Gillingham.
*Yachting*: soling class—Robert Cruikshank, Lawrence Smith and Simon Stewart.

## Barcelona Paralympics

The 1992 Paralympics in Barcelona for people with a physical disability attracted over 3,000 competitors from 86 countries. The British team won 128 medals—40 gold, 47 silver and 41 bronze—and finished third in the overall medals table behind the United States and Germany. This is the same position that Britain occupied in the Seoul Paralympics in 1988, when it gained 182 medals, 62 of them gold. Britain's most successful performers in Barcelona were Christopher Holmes, winner of six golds in swimming events in the partially-sighted category, and Tanni Grey, who won four gold medals in the wheelchair sprints.

Britain's swimming and athletics squads won 22 and 15 gold medals respectively, with Britain's other gold medals coming in judo, shooting and table tennis. British competitors also won medals in powerlifting, fencing and weightlifting. Britain's most successful team overall was the swimming squad, which won exactly half of Britain's total number of medals in all events and finished second to the United States in the swimming medals table.

## Madrid Paralympics

The inaugural Paralympics for people with learning difficulties took place in Madrid in September 1992. Competitions were held in five sports—athletics, swimming, basketball, soccer and table tennis. The British team was among the largest delegations, with

100 competitors, and won a total of 11 medals—two gold, four silver and five bronze. Britain finished tenth out of the 23 nations that took part. Australia topped the medals table, with Iceland second and Sweden third.

## World Student Games

In 1991 the 16th World Student Games—Universiade XVI—were held in Sheffield and attracted 5,500 competitors from 110 countries. Four new sports arenas were built in preparation for the Games, at a cost of £147 million, including the 25,000-capacity Don Valley Stadium, where the athletics events were held. Britain won a total of 14 medals—four gold, five silver and five bronze—and finished in ninth position in the overall medals table behind the United States and the People's Republic of China.

## Commonwealth Games

The 14th Commonwealth Games were held in Auckland, New Zealand, in 1990, attracting a record 55 nations from the British Commonwealth. As in previous Games, Britain was represented by four national teams. The most successful of these was England, which won a total of 129 medals (47 gold, 40 silver and 42 bronze) and finished second in the overall medals table behind Australia. Wales finished in sixth position, with a total of 25 medals, and Scotland came in eighth place, winning 22 medals. Northern Ireland won nine medals and finished in tenth position in the medals table.

The first Games were held in Hamilton, Canada, in 1930, when they were known as the British Empire Games. Since then the Games have been held in Canada on a further two occasions, in

Australia three times, in New Zealand on three occasions, in Scotland twice, and once in England, Wales and Jamaica. The last Games to be held in Britain were the 1986 Games, which were hosted by Edinburgh. The 1994 Games are to be held in Victoria, Canada, and the 1998 Games in Kuala Lumpur, Malaysia.

## Olympic Bid by Manchester

Manchester's bid to stage the 2000 Olympic Games was officially launched by the Prime Minister in February 1993. The bid received the full backing of the Government, but failed to win sufficient support from the International Olympic Committee, which announced in September 1993 that Sydney had been chosen to host the Games in preference to bids from Peking, Manchester, Berlin and Istanbul. Manchester had previously made an unsuccessful bid for the 1996 Olympics awarded to Atlanta.

Despite losing the bid, Manchester will still benefit from the construction of two major new facilities—an indoor arena and an indoor velodrome. The arena will be suitable for a wide range of sports, including boxing, football, ice skating and ice hockey, as well as being an ideal venue for pop concerts and a range of other events. The indoor velodrome is due for completion in 1994 and will become Britain's first indoor cycling centre. Both facilities have been assisted by government grants of £35 million and £8 million respectively.

# A to Z of Popular Sports and Pastimes

Some of the major sports in Britain, many of which were invented by the British, are described below. Additional information on these and other sports not covered in this chapter can be found in *A Digest of Sports Statistics for the UK*, published by the Sports Council (see Further Reading).

The increased provision of sports centres has improved opportunities for participating in indoor sports, such as basketball, volleyball, and squash, and almost all outdoor sports have continued to gain in popularity. Sportsmen and women may be professionals (paid players) or amateurs. Some sports, such as hockey and rowing, are amateur, but in others the distinction between amateur status and professional status is less strictly defined, or does not exist.

## Angling

One of the most popular countryside sports is angling, of which there are three main types: coarse, game and sea. Coarse fishing usually takes place on the slower reaches of rivers and on lakes and ponds, with game fishing on faster flowing rivers. Coarse fish include all indigenous freshwater fish other than salmonids or game fish (salmon, sea trout, brown and rainbow trout). Sea fishing has three main forms: angling from the shore or jetties; inshore fishing (within about 5 km of the shore); and deep sea fishing.

Angling is an overwhelmingly male sport, with an estimated ten times as many male as female participants among Britain's  4 million anglers. Many fish for salmon and trout, particularly in the rivers and lochs of Scotland and in Wales. In England and Wales the most widely practised form of angling is for coarse fish, such as pike, perch, carp, tench and bream. Separate organisations represent game, coarse and sea fishing clubs in England, Wales, Scotland and Northern Ireland.

The National Federation of Anglers in England organises national championships for coarse fishing and enters a team in the world angling championships. England won the world team event in 1987, 1988 and 1991 and the individual title in 1989, 1990 and 1991.

## Association Football

The game of football developed in the English public schools during the 19th century, and the first set of rules which form the basis of modern football was drawn up in 1862. The game quickly became professional and is now the largest spectator sport and one of the most popular participation sports.

Association football is controlled by separate football associations in England, Wales, Scotland and Northern Ireland. In England 340 clubs are affiliated to the English Football Association (FA) and more than 42,000 clubs directly through regional or district associations. The FA, founded in 1863, and the Football League, founded in 1888, were both the first of their kind in the world.

In England and Wales a major change occurred in August 1992 when a new FA Premier League was started, comprising 22 clubs. The remaining 70 full-time professional clubs play in three main divisions run by the Football League. In Scotland there are three divisions, with 38 clubs, which play in the Scottish Football

League. From 1994–95 the League will be increased to 40 clubs divided into four divisions, each with ten clubs. In Northern Ireland, 16 semi-professional clubs play in the Irish Football League. During the season, which lasts from August until May, over 2,000 English League matches are played; total attendances reached over 20 million in 1991–92. The requirements for all-seated accommodation at League football grounds are described on p. 56.

The major annual knock-out competitions are the FA Challenge Cup and the Coca-Cola Cup (the League Cup) in England, the Tennents Scottish Cup, the Scottish League Cup, the Irish Cup and the Welsh FA Cup. The finals are played at Wembley Stadium, London; at Hampden Park, Glasgow; at Windsor Park, or the Oval, Belfast; and at the National Stadium, Cardiff.

The Sports Councils have made grants available to a number of clubs and local authorities to enable them to modernise or expand football facilities in areas of urban deprivation. Grants for various improvements, such as all-weather pitches, are also made throughout Britain by the Football Associations and the Football Trust (see also p. 56). Between 1981–82 and 1988–89 the Football Trust allocated £10 million worth of grants to local authorities in England towards the provision and improvement of football facilities. This investment produced 290 new pitches, over 500 improved pitches, and some 250 new or improved changing pavilions.

England is to host the European Championships finals in 1996.

## Athletics

Amateur athletics is governed in Britain by the British Athletic Federation (BAF), which is affiliated to the International Amateur

Athletic Federation. The BAF is responsible for the selection of British teams for international events, and also administers coaching schemes. For the Olympic Games and the World and European championships one team represents Britain.

Athletics is attracting increasing numbers of participants, both men and women, in part because of the success of British competitors and the wide coverage of athletics events on television. In 1990 there were over 1,900 clubs affiliated to the governing bodies of athletics in Britain, with a membership of over 200,000. In recent years there has been a significant growth in mass participation events, such as marathons and half marathons. The London Marathon, which takes place every spring, attracted 25,000 runners in 1993, including leading athletes from a number of countries.

Britain has a long distinguished history in athletics, especially middle-distance events: in 1954, for example, Dr (now Sir) Roger Bannister became the first man to run a mile in under four minutes. More recently middle-distance world records have been held by Steve Ovett, Steve Cram and Sebastian Coe, who still holds the world record in both the 800 metres and the 1,000 metres.

Recent successes at international championships include two gold medals at the 1993 World Indoor Athletics Championships in Toronto—Yvonne Murray in the 3,000 metres and Tom McKean in the 800 metres—and three gold medals at the 1993 World Athletics Championships in Stuttgart. These were won by Linford Christie in the 100 metres, Colin Jackson in the 110 metres hurdles and Sally Gunnell in the 400 metres hurdles. Both Colin Jackson and Sally Gunnell broke the world record in their events, and Linford Christie recorded the fastest time by a European, just one-hundredth of a second outside the world record. Britain won a total of ten medals at the Championships and finished in fourth position in the overall medals table.

# Badminton

The sport of badminton takes its name from the Duke of Beaufort's country home, Badminton House, where the sport was first played in the 19th century. Badminton is organised by the Badminton Association of England and the Scottish, Welsh and Irish (Ulster branch) Badminton Unions. There are also English, Welsh and Scottish schools badminton associations.

Interest in badminton grew substantially during the 1970s and although formal club membership has declined in recent years, the game remains a widely popular activity. The decline in membership is partly due to the growth of multi-purpose leisure centres, which provide increased opportunities for participation outside of badminton clubs. Around 5 million people play badminton in Britain and there are over 5,000 clubs. Most of these do not own their own facilities but hire courts from local authority sports centres, schools and churches. There are approximately 2,500 facilities for badminton in England.

Badminton has become a popular spectator sport in the last decade, and major events, such as the All-England Championships, attract television coverage. In 1988 badminton was introduced as a demonstration sport in the Olympics, and in 1992 became a full Olympic sport. In 1993 the world championships were held at the National Indoor Arena in Birmingham.

# Basketball

The modern game of basketball was invented at the end of the 19th century in the United States and has become one of the world's most popular sports. In Britain there are about 1,000 registered clubs, and over 750,000 people participate in the game. The

English Basket Ball Association is the governing body of the sport in England, and there are similar associations in Wales, Scotland and Northern Ireland. These associations are all autonomous, affiliating separately to the International Basketball Federation. However, they are all represented on the British and Irish Basketball Federation, which acts as the co-ordinating body for Britain and the Irish Republic.

The leading clubs play in the National Basketball Leagues, and the main events of the year are the National Cup Finals and the Carlsberg Basketball Championships, staged in Sheffield and London respectively. Recreational basketball is currently being developed for young people, particularly in the inner cities. Mini-basketball and micro-basketball are versions of the game which have been developed for players under the age of 13.

Wheelchair basketball is played under the same rules, with a few basic adaptations, and in the same court as the running game. The Great Britain Wheelchair Basketball Association actively promotes the game, and there are about 35 teams playing in the National League.

In 1993 the English Basket Ball Association launched 'Mission 2000', which aims to make basketball the number one indoor sport in England by the year 2000.

## Bowls

Bowls has been played in Britain since the 13th century. The game of lawn bowls is played on a flat green. In the Midlands, the north of England and north Wales a variation called crown green bowls is played, so named because the centre of the green is higher than its boundaries. Lawn and crown green bowls are mainly summer games; in winter indoor bowls takes place on synthetic greens and is growing in popularity.

Once regarded as a pastime for the elderly, bowls is increasingly enjoyed by adults of all ages. In recent years the most notable increases have been in the number of women taking part, especially in England and Wales. Bowls is also popular among people with disabilities, especially the wheelchair bound and the visually handicapped.

About 4,000 lawn bowling clubs are affiliated to the English, Scottish, Welsh and Irish (Northern Ireland Region) Bowling Associations, which, together with Women's Bowling Associations for the four countries, play to the rules of the International Bowling Board. The British Crown Green Bowling Association is the governing body of crown green bowls, and has 3,200 affiliated clubs. The indoor game in England is administered by the English Indoor Bowling Association. Similar associations exist for Scotland, Wales and Northern Ireland and there are separate women's associations in each country.

At the world outdoor championships in Worthing in 1992 Tony Allcock won the singles gold and Scotland won the Leonard Trophy (the team title), together with gold medals in the pairs and the fours. In 1993 Richard Corsie won the world indoor singles championships in Preston for the third time in five years.

## Boxing

Boxing in its modern form dates from 1865, when the Marquess of Queensberry drew up a set of rules eliminating much of the brutality in prize-fighting and making skill the basis of the sport. Boxing is both amateur and professional, and in both strict medical regulations are observed.

All amateur boxing in England, including schoolboy, club, association and combined services boxing (in the armed forces), is controlled by the Amateur Boxing Association (ABA). There are separate associations in Scotland and Wales, and Northern Ireland forms part of the Irish Boxing Association. The associations organise amateur boxing championships as well as training courses for referees, coaches and others. Teams take part in international meetings, including the Commonwealth and Olympic Games, and European and World championships. The wearing of headguards is now compulsory in all British amateur competitions.

The number of clubs affiliated to the ABA peaked in the early 1980s, with a total of 900 clubs. Since 1982 the number of clubs has declined to 615. In Wales there has also been a slight decline in club affiliation, but in Scotland there has been a steady increase in affiliated clubs since 1985. In Northern Ireland the number of clubs affiliated to the Irish Association has remained at about the same level since the mid-1980s.

Professional boxing is controlled by the British Boxing Board of Control. The Board appoints inspectors, medical officers and representatives to ensure that regulations are observed and to guard against overmatching and exploitation. British boxing has a distinguished record and has had a number of European, Commonwealth and World champions. Britain currently has two super-middleweight world champions: Chris Eubank (World Boxing Organisation—WBO—champion) and Nigel Benn (World Boxing Council—WBC—champion). Britain has two other WBO champions—Steve Robinson (featherweight) and Paul Weir (straw-weight)—and one other WBC champion—Lennox Lewis (heavyweight).

## Chess

Recent coverage of Nigel Short's challenge for the world chess championship has helped to raise the profile of chess in Britain and to add to its growing popularity.

In January 1993 Nigel Short became the first Briton for over a century to win the right to challenge for the world chess championship by defeating Jan Timman in the world chess candidates' final. His world title match against Gary Kasparov, the world champion, was held at the Savoy Theatre in London from September to October 1993 and lasted for 21 of the scheduled 24 games. The match resulted in victory for Gary Kasparov by 12.5–7.5, with Nigel Short winning just one game in the contest.

Following a disagreement over prize money between the two players and the world governing body—the International Chess Federation (FIDE)—the contest was held under the auspices of the Professional Chess Association—a breakaway body formed by Kasparov and Short. A rival world championship final, staged by FIDE, between Jan Timman and the former world champion, Anatoly Karpov, took place at the same time in the Netherlands and Indonesia.

The governing bodies in Britain are the British Chess Federation (responsible for England and for co-ordinating activity among the home nations), the Scottish Chess Association and the Welsh and Ulster Chess Unions. Important domestic competitions include the British Championships, the National Club Championships, the County Championships and the Leigh Grand Prix. The Hastings Chess Congress, dating from 1895, is the world's longest running annual international chess tournament.

## Cricket

The basis of the modern laws of cricket was drawn up in 1835 by the Marylebone Cricket Club (MCC), which continues to frame the laws of the game today. The MCC and the Test and County Cricket Board (TCCB—representing first-class cricket) are based at Lord's cricket ground in north London, the administrative centre of the world game. Men's cricket in Britain is governed by the Cricket Council, consisting of representatives of the TCCB, the National Cricket Association (representing club and junior cricket), the Minor Counties Association, the Scottish Cricket Union, the Irish Cricket Union and the MCC.

Cricket is played in schools, colleges and universities, and amateur teams play weekly games in cities, towns and villages from late April to the end of September. Throughout Britain there is a network of league cricket, minor counties and club games.

The main competition in professional cricket is the Britannic Assurance County Championship, played by 18 first-class county teams. Recently, matches have been a mixture of three-day and four-day games, but from 1993 the competition has consisted of four-day matches only. There are also three one-day competitions: the Benson and Hedges Cup, the National Westminster Trophy and the AXA Equity & Law Sunday League. In the past 20 years one-day cricket has become increasingly popular and has produced additional revenue for the game.

Some of the best-supported games are the annual series of five-day Cornhill Insurance Test matches played between England and a touring team from Australia (which toured in 1993), India, New Zealand, Pakistan, South Africa, Sri Lanka or the West Indies in rotation each summer. A team representing England usually tours one or more of these countries in the British winter. Texaco Trophy one-day international games also attract large crowds. A World Cup competition takes place every four years, and England were runners–up to Pakistan in the 1992 final.

Cricket is also played by women and girls, the governing body being the Women's Cricket Association, founded in 1926. Women's cricket clubs have regular local fixtures, usually played at weekends, and many participate in the national league and club knock-out competitions. There are regular county matches as well as an area championship and a territorial competition. Test match series and a World Cup competition are played, with both major and minor cricketing nations taking part. In 1993 England won the Women's World Cup for the second time, defeating New Zealand in the final.

## Curling

Curling originated in Scotland, where it is usually played in teams of four and almost exclusively on purpose-built rinks indoors. The game involves sliding a granite stone towards a target area and each game lasts about two hours. The governing body of the sport in Scotland is the Royal Caledonian Curling Club, which was formed in 1838; it has over 21,000 members. Curling is played in 29 other countries, including England and Wales, and European and World championship competitions take place annually. Curling was a demonstration sport at the 1992 Winter Olympics and is scheduled for inclusion in the 1998 Olympics in Nagano, Japan.

## Cycling

There has been a resurgence of interest in cycling, both as a means of transport and as a sport and recreation, and this has led central and local government to make greater provision for cycling. Britain's first indoor velodrome is currently under construction in Manchester (see p. 67).

Cycling activities include road and track racing, cycle speedway, time-trialling, cyclo-cross (cross country racing), touring and bicycle moto-cross (BMX). In recent years there has been a significant growth in the use of all-terrain or mountain bikes.

The British Cycling Federation is the governing body for cycling as a sport, with over 1,000 affiliated clubs and 17,600 members. The Cyclists' Touring Club has 40,000 members and is the governing body for recreational and urban cycling and represents cyclists' interests in general. The Scottish Cyclists Union controls the sport in Scotland. In Northern Ireland the sport is controlled by the Ulster Cycling Federation and the Northern Ireland Cycling Federation.

Major cycling events in Britain include the Milk Race and the Kelloggs Tour of Britain, which take place annually. In 1994 Britain is to host two stages of the Tour de France. The Tour plans to arrive via the Channel Tunnel, which is scheduled to open in early 1994, and the two stages will take place between Dover and Portsmouth.

In July 1993 Chris Boardman set a new one-hour world record at the Bordeaux velodrome, when he became the first man to break through 52 kilometres. Another world record was broken by Graeme Obree, who lowered the 4,000 metres record when winning the world 4,000 m pursuit title at Hamar, Norway, in August 1993.

## Equestrianism

Equestrian activities include recreational riding, endurance riding, carriage driving, one- and three-day eventing and show jumping. The arts of riding and driving are promoted by the British Horse Society, which is concerned with the welfare of horses, road safety, riding rights of way and training. It runs the British Equestrian Centre at Stoneleigh in Warwickshire. With some 60,000 members, the Society is the parent body of the Pony Club and the Riding Club movements, which hold rallies, meetings and competitions culminating in annual national championships.

Leading horse trials, comprising dressage, cross-country and show jumping, are held every year at Badminton (Avon), Windsor (Berkshire), Gatcombe Park (Gloucestershire), Bramham (West Yorkshire), Burghley (Lincolnshire), Thurlestane Castle (Berwickshire), Blair Castle (Tayside) and Blenheim Palace (Oxfordshire).

Show jumping is regulated and promoted by the British Show Jumping Association, which has over 17,000 members and 2,900 shows affiliated to it. The major show jumping events each year include the Royal International Horse Show at Hickstead (West Sussex); the Horse of the Year Show at Wembley in London; the Olympia International Horse Show; and the Nations Cup and Derby meetings at Hickstead. Michael Whitaker is currently ranked number one in the world.

The authority responsible for equestrian competitions (other than racing) at international and Olympic level is the British Equestrian Federation, which co-ordinates the activities of the British Horse Society and the British Show Jumping Association. British equestrian teams have a good record in international competitions. At the World Equestrian Games held in Stockholm in 1990 Great Britain gained six medals: one gold, four silver and one bronze.

## Golf

Golf originated in Scotland, where for centuries it has carried the title of the Royal and Ancient Game. The oldest golf club in the world is the Honourable Company of Edinburgh Golfers, which was created in 1735. The Royal and Ancient Golf Club (R & A), the ruling authority of the sport for most of the world, is situated at St Andrews on the east coast of Scotland. Golf is played throughout

Britain and there are golf courses near most towns, a few of them owned by local authorities; there are about 1,900 golf courses in Britain.

The Golfing Union of Ireland and parallel unions in Wales, Scotland and England are the national governing bodies for men's amateur golf. These bodies co-operate with the R & A and are represented on the Council of National Golf Unions, which is the British co-ordinating body responsible for handicapping and organising international matches. Women's amateur golf is governed by the Ladies' Golf Union, which comprises a number of affiliated national bodies.

Club professional golf has its own administrative structure, and is governed by the Professional Golfers' Association (PGA) and the Women's PGA. For tournament professionals the governing bodies are the PGA European Tour and the Women Professional Golfers' European Tour Ltd.

There are Schools' Golf Associations in each of the home countries working to promote younger people's involvement. The Golf Foundation—a registered charity—has a wide responsibility for the junior game and is concerned with the provision of coaching and competitive opportunities for young people with a wide range of abilities and experience.

The main event of the British golfing year is the Open Championship, one of the world's leading tournaments. Other important events include the Walker Cup and Curtis Cup matches for amateurs, played between Great Britain and Ireland and the United States, and the Ryder Cup match for professionals, played between Europe and the United States. Among the leading British professional players are Nick Faldo and Ian Woosnam, both of whom have won a number of major tournaments. Nick Faldo won the Open in 1992 for the second time and is currently ranked number one in the world.

A number of championship golf courses are used for the staging of the British Open Championship. These include Muirfield, Royal Birkdale, Royal Lytham St Annes, St Andrews, Troon, Turnberry and Royal St George's at Sandwich, which staged the 1993 Open.

## Greyhound Racing

Greyhound racing is one of Britain's most popular spectator sports and takes place at 37 major tracks. Meetings are usually held three times a week at each track, with at least ten races a meeting. The rules for the sport are drawn up by the National Greyhound Racing Club, the sport's judicial and administrative body. The representative body is the British Greyhound Racing Board.

There are about 50 mainly small tracks which operate independently. Like the major tracks, they are licensed by local authorities.

The main event of the year is the Greyhound Derby run in June at Wimbledon Stadium, and worth £40,000 to the winning owner. Other major events include the Scottish Derby at Shawfield, Glasgow, the Greyhound Grand National at Hall Green, Birmingham, and the BBC Television Trophy. There is an annual challenge match, the Anglo-Irish International, run home and away at Sunderland and Dublin.

## Gymnastics

Gymnastics is divided into four main disciplines: artistic (or Olympic) gymnastics, rhythmic gymnastics, sports acrobatics and general gymnastics. Both men and women compete in artistic gymnastics, although the apparatus used differs. Men use the floor, pommel horse, rings, vault, parallel bars and horizontal bar, while women exercise on the vault, asymmetric bars, beam and floor. Rhythmic gymnastics is for women only and consists of routines performed to music with ribbon, balls, clubs, hoop and rope. Sports acrobatics is gymnastics with people rather than apparatus. General gymnastics is non-competitive and is available to all age groups and to people with special needs.

The governing body for the sport is the British Amateur Gymnastics Association (BAGA). Affiliated to the BAGA are the Welsh, Scottish and Northern Ireland Amateur Gymnastics Associations and the British Schools' Gymnastics Association. Over the past decade the number of clubs affiliated to the BAGA has nearly doubled. There are now about 1,000 clubs, with some 73,000 club members and a further 10,000 individual members of the BAGA. The sport is particularly popular with schoolchildren and young adults, and it has been estimated that between 3 and 4 million schoolchildren take part in some form of gymnastics every day. All the Associations actively promote the development of gymnastics among people with disabilities and offer special needs coaching from qualified tutors.

The BAGA has actively promoted the development of new specialist training centres and has close ties with the National Centre for Gymnastics at Lilleshall (see p. 30).

At the 1993 World Gymnastics Championships in Birmingham Neil Thomas became the first Briton to win a gymnastics medal at world level when he won the silver medal in the floor exercise.

## Highland Games

Scottish Highland Games cover a wide range of athletic competitions in addition to activities such as dancing and piping competitions. The oldest Highland Gathering dates back to the 14th century, while the Games in their modern form have existed since the early 19th century. The main events include running, cycling, throwing the hammer, tossing the caber and putting the shot. There are also pipe band and Highland dancing contests.

Over 70 gatherings of various kinds take place throughout Scotland, the most famous of which include the annual Braemar Gathering and the Argyllshire and Cowal Gatherings. Although most of the competitions are considered professional, there are many events in which amateurs can participate.

The Scottish Games Association (SGA) is the official governing body responsible for athletic sports and games at Highland and Border events in Scotland. The SGA is an association of committees rather than clubs and has more than 60 members. Each committee organises its own local games, and every year between 600 and 800 competitors from a number of countries participate.

The Games have become popular tourist attractions, and attendances total over 500,000 spectators each year.

## Hockey (Field and Indoor)

Variants of hockey have been played in Britain for at least five centuries. The modern game was started by the Hockey Association (of England), which was founded in 1886 and acts as the governing body for men's hockey. Parallel associations serve in Scotland, Wales and Ireland. All of these associations have responsibility for both the indoor and the outdoor game.

Media coverage of hockey and levels of sponsorship and participation have increased in recent years following the gold-medal winning success of the men's hockey team in the 1988 Olympics, and the bronze medal won by the women's team in the 1992 Olympics. There are now some 2,000 hockey clubs throughout Britain, many with junior sections. Large numbers of schools also play hockey, and some 500 are affiliated to the Hockey Association. Cup competitions and leagues exist at national, divisional or district, and club levels, both indoors (six-a-side) and outdoors, and there are regular international matches.

The controlling body of women's hockey in England is the All England Women's Hockey Association (founded in 1895), to which some 950 clubs and about 2,000 schools are affiliated; separate associations regulate the sport in Scotland, Wales and Ireland. League, county, club and school championships for both outdoor and indoor hockey are played annually in England. Regular international matches are played.

Traditionally hockey has been played on grass pitches, but recently there has been an increase in the use of artificial pitches, which allow a faster, more free-flowing game. All major competitions are now played on an artificial surface. The increase in the number of indoor sports centres over the past 20 years has helped indoor hockey become an important sport at both domestic and international level and to develop from its previous status as a training exercise for the outdoor game.

## Horse Racing

Horse racing takes two forms—flat racing and National Hunt (steeplechasing and hurdle racing). The main flat race season runs from late March to early November, but following the introduction of all-weather racing at two racecourses (Lingfield in 1989 and Southwell in 1990) flat race meetings now take place throughout the year. The Derby, run at Epsom, is the outstanding event in the flat racing calendar. Other classic races are: the Two Thousand Guineas and the One Thousand Guineas, both run at Newmarket; the Oaks (Epsom); and the St Leger (Doncaster).

The National Hunt season runs from late July/early August to early June. The most important meeting is the National Hunt Festival held at Cheltenham in March, which features the Gold Cup and the Champion Hurdle. The Grand National, run at Aintree, near Liverpool, is the world's best-known steeplechase and dates from 1837. In 1993 the race was declared void for the first time in its history following two false starts and the failure to recall all the runners. The Jockey Club subsequently set up a working group to consider improvements to the starting procedure, and has accepted the recommendations made by the group.

In June 1993 overall responsibility for the control of racing was passed from the Jockey Club to a new body—the British Horseracing Board. The 11-man Board consists of four members of the Jockey Club, four representatives of racehorse owners and race-courses, and three others representing the interests of jockeys, trainers, stable staff and racegoers. The Board is responsible for race planning, racecourse policy, the racing administration budget and consultation with the industry.

The Jockey Club retains an administrative role and is respon-sible for licensing, discipline, security and anti-doping measures.

Racing takes place from Monday to Saturday on most days of the year. In addition, since 1992 three race meetings have been held on a Sunday on an experimental basis, at Doncaster, Cheltenham and Lingfield. Owing to Britain's gambling laws, no on-course or off-course betting was allowed on these three days.

Britain has 59 racecourses and about 12,000 horses currently in training. The Government recently gave a boost to the racing and bloodstock industry when it announced in the March 1993 Budget that racehorse owners would in future be able to claim back the VAT (value added tax) payable on the purchase price of horses and on training fees. To enable the changes to go ahead, the Jockey Club is to remove the barriers to horse sponsorship and appearance money.

In April 1993 Peter Scudamore—the most successful National Hunt jockey of all time—announced his retirement after riding his 1,677th winner, 539 more than any other jockey.

## Ice Skating

Ice skating became popular in Britain in the late 19th and early 20th centuries and takes three main forms: figure skating (solo and pairs), ice dancing and speed-skating (indoor and outdoor). The governing body is the National Ice Skating Association (NISA) of Great Britain, founded in 1879 and affiliated to the International Skating Union.

Participation in ice skating is concentrated among the under-25s, and is one of the few sports that attracts more female than male participants. Both the numbers of individual members and ice skating clubs affiliated to the NISA rose considerably in the 1980s, possibly encouraged by British success at the Olympics and world championships. Since 1985 the number of affiliated clubs has risen from 65 to 105 in 1990.

Facilities for ice skating are mostly provided by the private sector and are situated in urban centres. There are over 70 rinks in Britain, almost half of which have opened since 1985.

British couples have won the world ice dance championship 17 times. Britain's most recent success in this event was achieved by Jayne Torvill and Christopher Dean, who won four consecutive world championships between 1981 and 1984 and a gold medal at the 1984 Winter Olympics in Sarajevo. The couple intend to return to international competition in 1994 following a rule change which permits professional skaters to return to amateur competition.

## Judo

Judo, an individual combat sport derived from the ancient Japanese art of ju-jitsu, is popular not only as a competitive sport and self-defence technique, but also as a means of general fitness training. Men and women take part in judo at all levels. An internationally recognised grading system is in operation through the sport's governing body, the British Judo Association.

Almost 1,000 judo clubs throughout Britain are registered with the Association, which is a founder member of the European Judo Union and a member of the International Judo Federation.

In the 1992 Olympics women's judo was included for the first time, and Britain won a total of four medals in the women's and men's events (see p. 64). Britain has won medals for judo at every Olympic Games since 1972.

At the 1993 World Championships Nicola Fairbrother won a gold medal in the under 56 kg category.

## Keep Fit

Various forms of movement and fitness activities are practised in Britain that include elements of eurhythmics, dance and aerobic exercise. The different organisations have varying emphases, but all are designed to develop greater physical and mental well-being. The Keep Fit Association, formed in 1956, receives funding from the Sports Council to promote physical fitness and a positive attitude to health in England. Its national certificated training scheme for keep fit teachers is recognised by local education authorities throughout Britain. Autonomous associations serve Scotland, Wales and Northern Ireland.

There are recognised governing bodies in other activities. In addition, there are large numbers of participants in circuit and weight training and informal fitness activities. The Sports Council plans to launch a National Exercise and Fitness Association in the near future (see p. 25).

## Martial Arts

A broad range of martial arts, mainly derived from Japan, the People's Republic of China, Taiwan, Hong Kong and Korea, has been introduced into Britain during the 20th century. There are recognised governing bodies responsible for their own activities in karate, ju-jitsu, aikido, Chinese martial arts, kendo, taekwondo and tang soo do. The most popular martial art is karate, with over 100,000 participants.

A review of martial arts organisations was undertaken in 1990 by the Sports Council. The review recommended that the Martial Arts Commission, which was established in 1977 as a control body for the governing bodies of martial arts, should become an advisory body and cease to be a membership organisation. However, the Commission rejected the Council's recommendations, choosing instead to remain as a membership body. As a result, an Advisory Group on Martial Arts was established by the Sports Council to provide a forum for discussing martial arts issues. The Council no longer recognises the Commission in any formal capacity.

## Motor-car and Motor-cycle Sports

Motor sports are gaining in popularity, both in spectating and participation. The main four-wheeled motor sports are motor racing, high-speed trials, autocross, rallycross, hill-climbing, rallying and karting. In motor racing the Formula One Grand Prix competition is the major form of the sport. It is estimated that there are over 100,000 car or kart competitors in Britain.

The governing body for four-wheeled motor sport is the RAC (Royal Automobile Club) Motor Sports Association. The Association issues licences for a variety of motoring competitions and organises the Network Q RAC Rally, an event in the contest for the World Rally Championship, and the British Grand Prix, which is held at Silverstone as part of the Formula One World Motor Racing Championship. In 1993 Britain also staged the Formula One European Grand Prix at Donington Park.

British car constructors, including Lotus, McLaren and Williams, have enjoyed outstanding successes in Grand Prix racing, and Britain has had seven world champion motor racing drivers. In 1992 Nigel Mansell won the world title, winning nine of the season's races. This brought his career wins in Formula One to 30, the most recorded by a British driver.

In 1993 Nigel Mansell won the IndyCar World Series Championship, which takes place in the United States and Australia. In so doing he became the first man to win the IndyCar title in his debut year and the only driver to win the Formula One world championship and IndyCar titles in successive years.

Damon Hill recorded three consecutive Grand Prix victories in 1993 in his first full season of Formula One racing.

Motor-cycle sports include road racing, moto-cross, grass track, speedway, trials, drag racing and sprint. It is estimated that there are between 40,000 and 50,000 competitive motor-cyclists in Britain.

The governing bodies of the sport are the Auto-Cycle Union in England and Wales, the Scottish Auto-Cycle Union and Motor Cycle Union of Ireland (in Northern Ireland). The major events of the year are the Isle of Man TT races, the British Road Race Grand Prix, the Ulster Grand Prix and other world championship events for trials, moto-cross, speedway, and grass and track racing. The Auto-Cycle Union provides off-road training by approved instructors for riders of all ages.

## Mountaineering

All forms of mountaineering, which includes hill-walking and rock-climbing, are growing in popularity. There are around 100,000 rock-climbers and 700,000 hill-walkers, whose representative body is the British Mountaineering Council; separate bodies serve Scotland and Ireland.

Britain can claim to have invented the sports of rock-climbing and alpine-climbing. The first recorded rock-climbs in Britain were made more than 100 years ago, and the Alpine Club, founded in 1857 and based in London, is the oldest mountaineering club in the world. British mountaineers have played a leading role in the exploration of the world's great mountain ranges. The best-known is Chris Bonington, who has climbed Everest and led many successful expeditions throughout the world. In May 1993 Rebecca Stephens became the first British woman to climb Everest.

Three National Centres for mountain activities are run by the Sports Councils: Plas y Brenin National Mountain Centre in Snowdonia (see p. 33); Glenmore Lodge, near Aviemore, in Scotland (see p. 34); and the Northern Ireland Centre for Outdoor Activities at Tollymore, County Down (see p. 35).

Popular areas for rock-climbing are south-west England, the Peak District of Derbyshire, the Lake District in north-west England, Wales and the Highlands of Scotland.

## Netball

Netball is derived from basketball, which came to Britain in the late 19th century. More than 60,000 adults play netball regularly in England and a further 1 million participants play in schools. The sport is played almost exclusively by women and girls both indoors and outdoors.

The All England Netball Association, formed in 1926, is the governing body in England. The English Schools' Netball Association is responsible for the sport in schools. Scotland, Wales and Northern Ireland have their own governing bodies. The number of clubs affiliated to the All England Association has increased considerably in recent years, from some 2,900 in 1985 to 6,075 in 1992.

## Rowing

Rowing is taught in many schools, colleges and rowing clubs throughout Britain. The main types of boats for rowing are single, pairs and double sculls, fours and eights. The governing body of the sport in England is the Amateur Rowing Association; similar bodies regulate the sport in Scotland, Wales and Northern Ireland. There are about 500 rowing clubs, and each year over 300 regattas and head races are held in Britain under Association rules.

The University Boat Race, between eight-oared crews from Oxford and Cambridge, has been rowed on the Thames almost every spring since 1836. The Head of the River Race, also on the

Thames, is the largest assembly of racing craft in the world, with more than 420 eights racing in procession. At the Henley Regatta in Oxfordshire, founded in 1839, crews from all over the world compete each July in various kinds of race over a straight course of 1 mile 550 yards (about 2.1 km).

The National Water Sports Centre at Holme Pierrepont, near Nottingham (see p. 31), has a rowing course of Olympic standard, as does Strathclyde Park in west-central Scotland.

At the World Rowing Championships in Roudnice, the Czech Republic, in September 1993 Britain won four gold medals: Gregory Searle, Jonathan Searle and Garry Herbert (coxed pairs); Steven Redgrave and Matthew Pinsent (coxless pairs); Peter Haining (lightweight single sculls); and the women's lightweight fours (Alison Brownless, Jane Hall, Annemarie Dryden and Tonya Williams).

## Rugby Football

Rugby football takes its name from Rugby School, in Warwickshire, where the sport is believed to have originated in 1823. Since the end of the 19th century the game has been played according to two different codes: rugby union (a 15-a-side game) is played by amateurs and rugby league (a 13-a-side game) by professionals as well as amateurs.

### Rugby Union

Rugby union is played under the auspices of the Rugby Football Union in England and parallel bodies in Wales, Scotland and Ireland. Important domestic competitions include the divisional and county championships in England; the league and national club knock-out competitions in England and Wales; and the National League and Inter-District Championships in Scotland.

The Five Nations Tournament between England, Scotland, Wales, Ireland and France is contested each year. In 1992 England completed the Grand Slam (beating all their opponents) for the second successive year. Overseas tours are undertaken by the national sides and by the British Lions, a team representing Great Britain and Ireland. Teams from 16 countries competed for the first World Cup competition in 1987. The final rounds of the second World Cup, in which 37 nations participated, were staged in Britain, Ireland and France in October and November 1991. England finished runners-up to Australia.

Seven-a-side rugby union has a strong following. Tournaments include the Middlesex Sevens, which is held every year at Twickenham, and every four years there is a World Cup. The inaugural World Cup was held in Edinburgh in April 1993. It attracted 24 entrants and was won by England.

**Rugby League**

Rugby league originated in 1895 following the breakaway from rugby union of a number of clubs in the north of England due to disagreement over the amateur status of the game. Rugby league has its own distinct set of rules, but it has kept many of the features of the union game. However, unlike rugby union, which is played nationally, it is concentrated in the north of England.

The governing body of the professional game is the Rugby Football League, which sends touring teams representing Great Britain to Australia, New Zealand and Papua New Guinea; annual matches are also played against France. The Challenge Cup Final, the major club match of the season, is played at Wembley Stadium in London.

The amateur game is governed by the British Amateur Rugby League Association. Matches between England and France are held each year and tours are arranged to Australia and New Zealand. A national league consisting of ten leading clubs was formed in 1986, and a second division in 1989.

## Skiing

Skiing takes place in Scotland from December to May and also at several English locations when there is sufficient snow. The five established winter sports areas in Scotland are Cairngorm, Glencoe, Glenshee, the Lecht and Aonach Mor, all of which have a full range of ski-lifts, prepared ski-runs and professional instructors.

There are over 150 artificial or dry ski-slopes located throughout Britain, which are in regular use. They are used extensively by clubs and schools as well as by skiers preparing for a holiday; over a third of British skiers learned to ski on these dry ski-slopes. Britain has nearly 300 ski clubs, with a membership of over 50,000. It is estimated that 1.5 million people take part in the sport.

The governing body of the sport is the British Ski Federation, and there are separate national councils for England, Scotland, Wales and Northern Ireland.

## Snooker and Billiards

The character of the present game of billiards was established in Britain at the end of the 17th century. Snooker, a more varied game invented by the British in India in 1875, has greatly increased in popularity and become a major spectator sport as a result of heavy television coverage of the professional tournaments. It is estimated that between 7 and 8 million people now play the game.

British players have an outstanding record in snooker and have dominated the major professional championships. The main tournament is the annual Embassy World Professional Championship, held in Sheffield. In the 1980s Steve Davis won the world title six times and in 1993 Stephen Hendry became world champion for the third time. Mike Russell won the World Professional Billiards Championship in 1991.

The controlling body for the non-professional game in England is the English Association for Snooker and Billiards. Scotland, Wales and Northern Ireland have separate associations. The World Professional Billiards and Snooker Association is responsible for professional players, and organises all world-ranking professional events. It also holds the copyright for the rules.

A growing number of women play snooker and billiards. Their representative body is the World Ladies' Billiards and Snooker Association, with around 250 members. A women's world snooker championship is played every year in London, and was won in 1993 for the sixth time by Allison Fisher. The World Masters event, staged in Birmingham, embraces men's and women's singles and doubles as well as mixed doubles. The Embassy World Professional Championship was opened to women in 1992.

## Squash

Squash derives from the game of rackets, which was invented at Harrow School in the 1850s. Separate governing bodies are responsible for the sport in England, Wales, Scotland and Ireland. The governing body in England is the Squash Rackets Association, formed in 1989 when the separate men's and women's associations amalgamated. The main tournament is the British Open Championship.

Squash enjoyed a period of very rapid growth during the 1970s and remains a popular sport. There are nearly 9,000 squash courts in England, and the estimated number of players in Britain is almost 1 million. The main providers of facilities are member clubs, commercial organisations and local authorities, which provide squash facilities in many sports centres. Local authority centres play an important role in introducing the sport to new players, especially young people.

## Sub-aqua

Sub-aqua activities include scuba diving, snorkel diving, wreck and reef exploration, underwater photography, marine life studies and nautical archaeology. There has been a large increase in the popularity of the sport over the last ten years.

The British Sub-Aqua Club is the governing body for all underwater activities. It promotes safe training for both sport and scientific divers and is also involved in marine conservation. The Club is the largest of its kind in the world, with over 47,000 members and more than 1,250 branches in Britain and overseas.

Training in all aspects of diving safely is mainly carried out by British Sub-Aqua Club branches and schools, all of which have to use nationally qualified instructors. Early stages of training are carried out in swimming pools, so the future growth of the sport depends very much on pool time being made available by local authorities.

## Swimming

Swimming is considered to be one of the most beneficial forms of exercise and attracts people with a wide range of abilities from all age groups. It is enjoyed by millions of people both as a popular recreational activity and as a competitive sport.

More specialised forms of the sport have developed their own competitive structure. These include diving (platform and spring-board), water polo (invented in Britain in the second half of the 19th century) and synchronised swimming.

All forms of competitive swimming are governed by the Amateur Swimming Association (ASA) in England and by similar associations in Scotland and Wales. These three associations combine to form the Amateur Swimming Federation of Great Britain, which acts as the co-ordinating body for the selection of Great Britain teams and the organisation of international competitions. Northern Ireland forms part of the Irish Amateur Swimming Association.

Instruction and coaching are provided by qualified teachers and coaches who hold certificates awarded mainly by the ASA, to which some 1,700 clubs are affiliated. Competitive and recreational swimming are almost entirely dependent on subsidised local authority provision.

The most advanced aquatic facility in the world was opened in 1991 at Ponds Forge, Sheffield. The pool contains separate leisure and diving pools as well as a 50 m competition pool. It is run by the local authority and is intended for community use as well as an international venue. In 1993 it hosted the European Championships, at which Britain won a total of 12 medals, including a gold for Nick Gillingham in the 200 metres breaststroke. The British team finished sixth in the overall medals table.

Mark Foster holds the short-course (25-metre pool) world record for the 50 metres freestyle.

## Table Tennis

The game of table tennis developed in Britain in the latter half of the 19th century, becoming an Olympic sport in 1988. In addition to being one of the most popular indoor sports for young people, it is played by a broad age range of adults, with men significantly outnumbering women. Requiring relatively simple and inexpensive equipment, table tennis is played in sports centres, schools, youth clubs and private clubs. Table tennis is also a major recreational and competitive sport for people with disabilities, and the British Sports Association for the Disabled organises major table tennis championships for its members. The sport is currently undergoing a major development programme in England entitled Focus Sport, which aims to introduce new players to the game, to improve facilities and the quality of training, and to give support to voluntary leagues and clubs.

The governing body for men's and women's table tennis in England is the English Table Tennis Association, to which some 4,500 clubs are affiliated. There are separate governing bodies in Scotland, Wales and Northern Ireland. The English Schools Table Tennis Association is also very active, particularly with competitions. In April 1993 it hosted the World Schools Games in Birmingham.

In March/April 1994 England will host the European Table Tennis Championships at the National Indoor Arena in Birmingham. Approximately 50 countries are expected to be represented.

## Tennis

The modern game of tennis originated in England in 1872 and the first championships were played at Wimbledon in 1877. The controlling body in Great Britain is the Lawn Tennis Association (LTA—founded in 1888), to which the Welsh and Scottish LTAs are affiliated. Northern Ireland forms part of Tennis Ireland (formerly the Irish Lawn Tennis Association). In 1992 there were over 2,400 clubs affiliated to the LTA. Tennis was incorporated into the Olympic programme in 1988.

The main event of the year is the annual Wimbledon fortnight, one of the four 'Grand Slam' tournaments. This draws large crowds, with the ground at the All England Club accommodating around 30,000 spectators, and the tournament is covered extensively on television. Prize money has increased dramatically over the last decade and totalled over £5 million in 1993 (see Table 3). Since 1980 the All England Club has donated almost £100 million to the LTA for the development of the game.

**Table 3: Wimbledon Prize Money and Profits Since 1980**

| Year | Prize Money | Men's Singles Champion | Women's Singles Champion | Pre-tax Surplus to LTA £ |
|---|---|---|---|---|
| 1980 | 293,464 | 20,000 | 18,000 | 20,810 |
| 1983 | 978,211 | 66,600 | 60,000 | 2,751,154 |
| 1986 | 2,119,780 | 140,000 | 126,000 | 6,200,848 |
| 1989 | 3,133,749 | 190,000 | 171,000 | 9,202,486 |
| 1992 | 4,416,820 | 265,000 | 240,000 | 14,300,000 |
| 1993 | 5,048,450 | 305,000 | 275,000 | 16,400,000 |

There are national and county championships and national competitions for boys' and girls' schools. Short tennis was introduced in recent years to encourage children aged five and over to take part in the sport. The game uses a court of similar size to a badminton court and is played in over 3,000 schools and in leisure centres. In all, there are some 3 million people who play tennis in Britain.

The main providers of tennis courts are local authorities, private clubs and education authorities. In the last decade there has been a significant increase in the number of indoor courts, mainly as a result of the Sports Council's Indoor Tennis Initiative (see p. 12).

British tennis recently showed signs of a revival when James Baily won the 1993 junior singles championship at the Australian Open, becoming the first British male to win a singles Grand Slam title for 28 years. Another British player to have achieved success in recent years is Jamie Delgado, who in 1991 won the under-14 Orange Bowl title, a prestigious junior event.

## Tenpin Bowling

Modern tenpin bowling was developed in the United States during the 19th century. The first centre in Britain opened in 1960. During the 1980s the sport increased in popularity, and it is estimated that there are now some 4.8 million people who take part in tenpin bowling every year in Britain. Over 200 national tournaments take place each year and there is an annual National Championship, which attracts up to 1,500 players. Players participate in team, doubles and singles events.

Most of Britain's 200 indoor bowling centres are owned by private companies. Tenpin bowling is particularly suitable for people with disabilities, and many centres have facilities for disabled participants. More than 30,000 people belong to the sport's governing body, the British Tenpin Bowling Association, through over 700 nationwide leagues.

## Volleyball

Volleyball was established in Britain in the 1950s, having first been played in the United States at the end of the 19th century. The number of registered players in Britain grew substantially in the 1980s, with men at first far outnumbering women; today, of the total of 25,000 registered players, about 11,000 are women. Volleyball is popular among schoolchildren and university and college students. Mini-volley is a version of the game adapted for children under 13. Volleyball is normally played in indoor sports halls, but it can also be played outside. Beach volleyball, for example, is becoming increasingly popular.

The English Volleyball Association and parallel associations in Scotland, Wales and Northern Ireland act as the sport's governing bodies. The British Volleyball Federation, comprising one member from each of the four home countries, meets regularly to discuss interests of common concern regarding volleyball within Britain and to draw up policies.

## Yachting

Yachting comprises sailing, powerboating and windsurfing on both inland and offshore waters. Sailing includes offshore cruisers, offshore racers, keelboats, catamarans and dinghies. The sport expanded considerably in the latter half of the 19th century when the modern form of yacht racing was started, with special right of way rules and handicapping.

The racing classes of sailing boats include dinghy, keelboat and catamaran classes, as well as windsurfers. Offshore racing involves yachts capable of supporting their crew overnight or longer. Races take place between one-design classes or under handicap, which provides level racing for boats of different size and shape. The most well-known ocean races include the Whitbread Round the World Yacht Race and the Fastnet Race. The latter is sailed every two years from Cowes, Isle of Wight, round the Fastnet Rock off the south-west coast of Ireland and back to Plymouth. Another popular event is the annual Cowes Regatta, which is organised by the Cowes combined clubs.

About 60,000 dinghies and keelboats race regularly on inshore and inland waters either in class fleets or in different classes under handicap racing. Powerboating has two main forms: inland circuit racing and offshore racing. Annual powerboating events take place all over the country, including Liverpool and Cardiff docks, attracting crowds of up to 50,000.

The Royal Yachting Association is the governing body for all yachting in Britain and has about 70,000 members and 1,500 clubs and classes. It is estimated that about 3 million people participate in yachting in Britain.

# Addresses

## Government Departments

Department of National Heritage, 2–4 Cockspur Street, London SW1Y 5DH. Tel: 071 211 6000.

Northern Ireland Office, Stormont Castle, Belfast BT4 3ST. Tel: 0232 763255.

The Scottish Office, New St Andrew's House, Edinburgh EH1 3TD. Tel: 031 556 8400.

Welsh Office, Cathays Park, Cardiff CF1 3NQ. Tel: 0222 825111.

Department for Education, Sanctuary Buildings, Great Smith Street, London SW1P 3BT. Tel: 071 925 5000.

Home Office, Queen Anne's Gate, London SW1H 9AT. Tel: 071 273 3000.

## Sports Councils

The Sports Council, 16 Upper Woburn Place, London WC1H 0QP. Tel: 071 388 1277.

Sports Council for Northern Ireland, House of Sport, Upper Malone Road, Belfast BT9 5LA. Tel: 0232 381222.

Scottish Sports Council, Caledonia House, South Gyle, Edinburgh EH12 9DQ. Tel: 031 317 7200.

Sports Council for Wales, National Sports Centre, Sophia Gardens, Cardiff CF1 9SW. Tel: 0222 397571.

**National Sports Centres**

Bisham Abbey National Sports Centre, Nr Marlow, Buckinghamshire SL7 1RT. Tel: 0628 476911.

Crystal Palace National Sports Centre, Ledrington Road, Norwood, London SE19 2BB. Tel: 081 778 0131.

Holme Pierrepont National Water Sports Centre, Adbolton Lane, Holme Pierrepont, Nottingham NG12 2LU. Tel: 0602 821212.

Lilleshall Hall National Sports Centre, Nr Newport, Shropshire TF10 9AT. Tel: 0952 603003.

Plas y Brenin National Centre for Mountain Activities, Capel Curig, Gwynedd LL24 0ET. Tel: 069 04 214.

Plas Menai National Watersports Centre, Llanfairisgaer, Caernarfon, Gwynedd LL5 IUE. Tel: 0248 670964.

The Welsh Institute of Sport, Sophia Gardens, Cardiff CF1 9SW. Tel: 0222 397571.

The Scottish National Sports Centre—Cumbrae, Inverclyde, Largs KA40 8RW. Tel: 0475 674666.

The Scottish National Sports Centre—Glenmore Lodge, Aviemore PH22 1QU. Tel: 0479 86256.

The Scottish National Sports Centre—Inverclyde, Largs KA30 8RW. Tel: 0475 674666.

The Northern Ireland Centre for Outdoor Activities, Tollymore, Bryansford, County Down, Northern Ireland. Tel: 03967 22158.

**Other Official Organisations**

British Olympic Association, 1 Wandsworth Plain, London SW18 1EH. Tel: 081 871 2677.

British Paralympic Association, Delta Point, Room G13A, 35 Wellesley Road, Croydon, Surrey CR9 2YZ. Tel: 081 666 4556.

British Sports Association for the Disabled, Solecast House, 13–27 Brunswick Place, London N1 6DX. Tel: 071 490 4919.

British Waterways Board, Greycaine Road, Watford WD2 4JR. Tel: 0923 226422.

Central Council of Physical Recreation, Francis House, Francis Street, London SW1P 1DE. Tel: 071 828 3163.

Countryside Commission, John Dower House, Crescent Place, Cheltenham GL50 3RA. Tel: 0242 521381.

The Foundation for Sport and the Arts, P.O. Box 666, Liverpool L69 7JN. Tel: 051 524 0235.

National Play Information Centre, First Floor, 359–361 Euston Road, London NW1 3AL. Tel: 071 383 5455.

National Coaching Foundation, 114 Cardigan Road, Headingley, Leeds LS6 3BJ. Tel: 0532 744802.

National Playing Fields Association, 25 Ovington Square, London SW3 1LQ. Tel: 071 584 6445.

National Sports Medicine Institute, c/o St Bartholomew's Medical College, Charterhouse Square, London EC1M 6BQ. Tel: 071 251 0583.

Northern Ireland Council of Physical Recreation, House of Sport, Upper Malone Road, Belfast BT9 5LA. Tel: 0232 381222.

Scottish Natural Heritage, 12 Hope Terrace, Edinburgh EH9 2AS. Tel: 031 447 4784.

Scottish Sports Association, Caledonia House, South Gyle, Edinburgh EH1 3TD. Tel: 031 339 8785.

Sports Aid Foundation, 16 Upper Woburn Place, London WC1H 0QN. Tel: 071 387 9380.

United Kingdom Sports Association for People with Learning Disability, Solecast House, 13–27 Brunswick Place, London N1 6DX. Tel: 071 250 1100.

Welsh Sports Association, Sophia Gardens, Cardiff CF1 9SW. Tel: 0222 397571.

Women's Sports Foundation, Wesley House, 4 Wild Court, London WC2B 5PN. Tel: 071 831 7863.

# Further Reading

£

| | | | |
|---|---|---|---|
| *Building on Ability: Sport for People with Disabilities.* Available from the Department of National Heritage | Department of Education and Science. | 1989 | Free |
| *Coaching Matters.* | Sports Council | 1991 | Free |
| *Community Use of Primary Schools.* | Sports Council | 1992 | Free |
| *A Countryside for Sport.* | Sports Council | 1992 | Free |
| *A Digest of Sports Statistics for the UK* (third edition). ISBN 1 872158 25 0. | Sports Council | 1991 | 25.00 |
| *The Economic Impact of Sport in the United Kingdom in 1990.* ISBN 1 87215 806 4. | Sports Council | 1992 | 25.00 |
| *Fair Play in Sport—A Charter.* | Central Council of Physical Recreation | 1991 | Free |
| *The Hillsborough Stadium Disaster.15 April 1989. Inquiry by the Rt Hon Lord Justice Taylor. Final Report.* Home Office. Cm 962. ISBN 0 10 109622 4. | HMSO | 1990 | 10.50 |

£

*A National Lottery Raising Money for
Good Causes.* Cm 1861.
ISBN 0 10 118612 6.                  HMSO 1992   3.80

*Networking for Women's Sport.*         Women's
                            Sports Foundation 1992   3.00

*Play Ground Safety*       Department of National
*Guidelines.*                     Heritage 1992   Free

*Sport and Active Recreation.*
ISBN 0 85522 409 6. Available      Department
from the Department of National    of Education
Heritage                        and Science. 1991   Free

*A Sporting Double: School and
Community.* ISBN 0 11 270774 2.      HMSO 1991   5.95

*Sport in the Nineties: New Horizons.*    Sports
                                 Council 1993  10.00

*UK Compendium of Sport: The Directory*   Sports
*of Governing Bodies of Sport.*        Council 1993   Free

*Women and Sport: A Consultative Document.*  Sports
                                 Council 1992   Free

*Young People and Sport.*              Sports
                                 Council 1993   Free

## Periodical Publications
(annual unless otherwise stated)
*The Sports Council Annual Report.*

*The Scottish Sports Council Annual Report.*
*The Sports Council for Wales Annual Report.*
*The Sports Council for Northern Ireland Annual Report.*
*Sport and Leisure: The Magazine of the Sports Council.*
(Bi-monthly.)
*Women and Sport.* (Quarterly.)Women's Sports Foundation

# Index

Written by Reference Services,
Central Office of Information.

Printed in the UK for HMSO.
Dd.297717, 2/94, C30, 56–6734, 5673